KNOW YOUR ONIONS

GARDENING
PUZZLE
AND
QUIZ BOOK

An exclusive edition for

for all your gift books and gift stationery

This edition first published in Great Britain in 2018
by Allsorted Ltd, Watford, Herts, UK
WD19 4BG

© Susanna Geoghegan Gift Publishing

Author and compiler: Fiona Thornton
Cover design: Milestone Creative

ISBN: 978-1-911517-53-5
Printed in China

· INTRODUCTION ·

After a hard day in the garden, there's nothing better than putting your feet up and relaxing with a nice cup of tea or a glass of something chilled. But while your body needs to rest, you can put your mind to work with this collection of garden-themed puzzles. From simple conundrums to fiendish wordsearches, and from cryptic crosswords to good old-fashioned quiz questions and much more, this book is sure to exercise those little grey cells and test your gardening knowledge – and may even inspire you with some new gardening ideas along the way.

· GENERAL KNOWLEDGE 1 ·

1. Only one British native tree is named after the month in which it blooms, but it also has another common name. By what two names is it known?

2. What is the common name for *Ilex*?

3. Of which fruit do the leaves of *Melissa officinalis* smell?

4. What flower is named after botanist Dr Leonard Fuchs?

5. What are the leaves of ferns called?

6. True or false? Asparagus is a member of the lily family.

7. What are the four ingredients of loam?

8. What is the term for covering soil with a layer of organic or inorganic matter to prevent weeds?

9. When was the RHS Chelsea Flower Show first held?
   a) 1948
   b) 1897
   c) 1913
   d) 1960

10. Witch hazel is used in many health and beauty products. What is its botanical name?

11. Which king is traditionally credited with creating the Hanging Gardens of Babylon?

12. Which popular garden tree with hanging yellow flowers has poisonous seeds?

13. In which decade of the 19th century was the Royal Horticultural Society founded as the Horticultural Society of London?

14. The garden of the National Trust's Waddesdon Manor in Buckinghamshire surrounds a property built in the style of a French chateau. Which famous banking family built the house and created the gardens in the 19th century?

15. What is unique about hydrophytic plants?

16. What is made from the dried leaves of *Camellia sinensis*?

17. Where might you find blanket weed growing?

18. To which fruit does the caterpillar of the codling moth cause damage?

19. Which bird is the most common visitor to the British garden?

20. According to folklore, when should beans be planted to bring good luck?

· BEAUTIFUL BLOOMS ·

```
H A T P K N O C R I U U N D I
J Y R M D I L Z O C T K E A M
Y U A P V E G U S D R I T F W
X N R C M Z R L E E E T J F A
I U O A I U C A R N A T I O N
Z R T E U N I B M T L E F D E
E I I R P T T N U W L K B I M
S I F S B N X H A O E V A L O
F R E E S I A J R R B R N Y N
N E M A L C Y C P R E J D P E
A I L H A D H I X B U G M P N
I Q Q H T I L U R F L N K O V
H Y E V D U V E B H B L E P M
Q S Q P T W G G O L A S T E R
X V C N U W B M Q Q D J X H E
```

Iris   Tulip   Hyacinth   Geranium
Peony   Carnation   Daffodil   Aster
Gerbera   Orchid   Anemone   Bluebell
Poppy   Freesia   Clematis
Rose   Dahlia   Cyclamen

· WORD LADDER 1 ·

B	E	A	N
1			
2			
3			
4			
C	A	N	E

Change the word from BEAN to CANE. Change one letter each time, so that each step forms a new word.

· HERBAL ANAGRAMS ·

RANCID ORE _____

O! AN OGRE _____

PEN PERT IMP _____

MR YO'S EAR _____

GNAT ROAR _____

I'M CALM HOE _____

CAGE NAIL _____

LONG SMEARS _____

· IN THE SHADE ·

The eleven clues in italics (which have no definition) yield
an answer which is the name of a plant which likes shade.

Across

1. Some aspic leaves split (6)
4. Swinging weight is lump remoulded around end of rope, nudged delicately underneath first of all (8)
10. *Uncle? A lad reformed!* (9)
11. Strong winds girl suffers initially (5)
12. Main artery turning back in that road (5)
13. Hunts etc all over the place, seeking, initially, old jokes (9)
14. Variety of 25 Across, mostly elegant, wilts finally (7)
16. Mud left behind by flowing water, settles in layers thinly first of all (4)
19. Musical instrument found in Bantu band (4)
21. My tyres are shredded – something very puzzling (7)
24. The soul in disarray? Most irreligious (9)
25. *Has to reorder* (5)
26. Making use of you and me in gardening first of all (5)

27. Fails to notice concerning comeliness (9)
28. Means Dave gets rid of leader and is very angry (8)
29. *Reconstitute soil round ends of convex pergola* (6)

Down

1. *Cancel my rearrangement* (8)
2. Part of garden, large drain made bigger (8)
3. *Very interesting news concerning auditors, first of all* (5)
5. If you rub with one of these, you could start again with a clean sheet! (7)
6. *Fingers grasp front half of alisma* (9)
7. *Leaders of labour in lethargic industries urge militancy* (6)
8. Treat badly leader of musicians over issue being presented in a different way (6)
9. *Dinner menu has calorific gateau portions last of all* (6)
15. *Quail flying around, for example, I admire initially* (9)
17. Sewage storage tank cops lose in chaos (8)

18. Roads built round towns by stupid people after start of project (8)
20. *Change one name* (7)
21. Bother changing top for Mum (6)
22. *Young bear captured by Alaskan ursine alliance initially* (6)
23. The hyacinths, replanted in vases everywhere first of all, grow strong and healthy (6)
25. Spiral shape almost held nine in Roman times (5)

· THE GARDEN YEAR ·

JANUARY
This is the time to start sprouting potatoes.
What is this process called?

FEBRUARY
You might plant hellebores this month. By what
common names are they known?

MARCH
Two saints' days fall in this month. Name a plant you
might associate with each of them.

APRIL
National Beanpole Week falls in this month. Which
wood are traditional beanpoles made of?

MAY
If you're planting out tomatoes this month, you might
consider companion plants to deter pests. Name a
flowering plant that you might choose for this purpose.

JUNE
Keep an eye on your lettuces! As the days get longer
they can be prone to flowering and going to seed. What
is this process called?

JULY
St Swithin's Day falls on the 15th. Why would
gardeners be anxious about the weather on this date?

AUGUST

This is a good time to propagate rhododendrons. You can do this by bending a shoot down to the ground, cutting a nick in it, and weighting it down in the soil to root. What is this technique called?

SEPTEMBER

Now is the time to start planting spring bulbs such as daffodils. There are thirteen 'divisions' or types of daffodil, the most common being the type with a cup longer than the petals. What is this type known as?

OCTOBER

Halloween brings October to an end. What is the record for the heaviest pumpkin ever grown?

a) 167 kg (368 lb)
b) 2,020 kg (4,453 lb)
c) 1,054 kg (2,323 lb)
d) 450 kg (992 lb)

NOVEMBER

At this time of year you might wrap grease bands around the trunks of your fruit trees. Why?

DECEMBER

Choose the gift that keeps on giving this Christmas by giving someone a *Hippeastrum* bulb. By what name is this plant better known?

· CAN'T SEE THE WOOD FOR THE TREES ·

The names of 18 trees are hidden in the grid. As you find them and cross them off, list them in the spaces below the grid.

R	O	W	E	G	R	L	K	V	M	L	E	V	Q	L
E	A	D	T	E	L	K	G	S	Q	Q	I	K	R	D
D	K	Z	D	M	T	B	E	E	C	H	E	A	K	H
L	T	L	A	L	D	U	T	H	C	G	L	J	A	O
A	E	P	X	J	R	X	N	I	H	P	J	W	F	L
W	L	W	R	S	J	W	K	T	O	A	T	M	J	L
E	K	O	G	O	P	I	G	P	S	H	Z	Y	U	Y
H	C	R	I	B	W	N	E	H	O	E	E	E	O	O
W	A	L	N	U	T	A	E	R	Y	W	H	V	L	O
V	O	C	T	S	W	N	N	P	M	T	P	C	W	C
R	O	F	O	Z	U	Y	Y	A	S	K	M	O	O	R
E	R	O	M	A	C	Y	S	Y	I	A	Z	F	L	L
S	G	A	G	Z	U	Z	H	Q	U	Y	L	H	L	T
O	I	J	K	H	H	G	O	O	M	V	U	L	I	K
W	P	G	M	G	S	R	I	T	P	A	M	S	W	K

_____   _____   _____   _____

_____   _____   _____   _____

_____   _____   _____   _____

_____   _____   _____

· PLUS ONE 1 ·

Each answer is an anagram of the one above, with one letter added. The final, unclued, answer is a plant, flower or shrub.

Organ of listening

Rip

Our planet

Part of a fireplace

· WORDFLOWER 1 ·

Using the letters in the flower, make as many words as you can of four or more letters. Each word must use the letter in the centre and no letter can be used more times than it appears in the flower. Use all nine letters to make the name of a flower or plant.

Goal:
a minimum of 25 words.

9-letter word

_ _ _ _ _ _ _ _ _

· **FLOWERS** ·

Across

1. Plant producing fruit before flower (5,8)
10. One French city can be included, that's weird (7)
11. Hit rump, crazy win (7)
12. Nancy meddled with part of young shoot (4)
13. Tree on the shore, say (5)
14. Flower girl (4)
15. Oddly heavy grass that has been dried (3)
17. Use manoeuvre after taking me back (6)
18. Flower suffering from poor drainage (8)
20. Negative denoted the rein (3)
21. We set about vegetable or flower (8)
22. Return cry with sex-appeal from bird (6)
23 and 27. Unsurprisingly it comes from conifer (3-4)
24. Flower girl (4)
26. Lit up fancy bulb (5)
27. See 23
30. OT book had a bio originally (7)
31. Gold put behind board in theatrical scene (7)
32. Wet container removed containing single flower (6,7)

Down

2. Chart in locker affected American tree (4,5)
3. Salmon-coloured flower (4)
4. Lady found 15 Across on pasture (6)
5. Absolute monarch's car damaged cart (8)
6. Flower girl (4)
7. Play times (5)
8. Shopkeeper's second space contains evergreen shrub (8,5)
9. After church Ryan's upset over the parent's bloomer (13)
13. Tree bark (3)
15. Innkeeper has a perennial plant (5)
16. This snake's tongue's a fern (5)
18. Journey to a district in India (3)
19. Modern rustic part of Hampshire (3,6)
20. Hen ran up round waterlily (8)
22. Twopence I included for seed (3)

23. Pugilistic part chief is tickled about (6)
25. Religious instructor crawled over one (5)
28. First sign I left of mud (4)
29. Scottish port getting round prohibition (4)

· FRUITY ·

1. What other name is sometimes given to the raspberry?

2. What is the name given to the study of grapes (usually for winemaking)?

3. What is the common name given to the natural thinning-out process of fruit, when trees shed some of their immature fruits early in the season, allowing the rest more space and nutrition to grow?

4. What is distinctive about the appearance of a kiwano melon?

5. Some fruits can be grown commercially in liquids, without soil. What is this method called?

6. Which came first, the use of the word 'orange' to describe a fruit or to describe the colour?

7. Which of the following is *not* a genuine fruit?
   a) Alligator apple
   b) Snake apple
   c) Monkey apple
   d) Elephant apple

8. 'Aprigold' is a dwarf tree variety producing which fruit?

9. Medlars benefit from 'bletting' before being eaten. What does this process involve?

10. Which south-east Asian fruit has a characteristically unpleasant smell, often described as 'decay' or 'rotten onions'?

11. What name is given to the fruit which is a cross between a grapefruit and a tangerine?

12. What colour are lingonberries?

13. Approximately how much water, as a percentage of its weight, does a watermelon contain?

14. Lancashire Lad is a variety of which soft fruit?

15. Which of these fruits is *not* native to North America?
a) Blueberry
b) Apple
c) Cranberry
d) Grape

16. Approximately how many seeds are on an average strawberry?

17. A loganberry is a cross between two berries – which two?

18. Which fruit merits its own museum in Belgium?
a) The apple
b) The orange
c) The strawberry
d) The pear

19. In which century were bananas first sold in London?

20. What is the other name for the fruit known as the Chinese gooseberry?

· STRUCTURES AND FEATURES ·

```
H E P D E H S T G Y I E D E I
S C G E B V R T Q C R S E C I
A W R Y R E K C O R V U C A S
L E O A L G N K D T T O K R L
L Z V L E G O C S I Q H I R D
O W I C X S X L H I E N N E D
J S O B S X U H A V L E G T N
T F Z I J I T O A B F E Z O O
F O U N T A I N H E K R B B P
F W A R B O U R N R Y G E O A
H O Y D Q Y R C O F E Z D O T
S N R W P I E T F R A M U O I
T I Q S R T T G R G C U M E O
B A C B P D U X S G H D Z U W
P D I W N X W X T M P S N N S
```

Shed	Bench	Pond	Fountain
Gazebo	Birdbath	Patio	Fence
Pergola	Arch	Obelisk	Arbour
Summerhouse	Trellis	Greenhouse	
Decking	Rockery	Terrace	

· BAGGAGE HANDLING ·

Maggie and Joe were walking through the garden centre, carrying bags of bulbs and potting compost, when Joe began to complain that his load was too heavy. 'I don't know what you're moanning about,' said Maggie, 'because if you gave me one of your bags I'd have twice as many as you, and if I gave you just one we'd both have the same number.' How many bags was each of them carrying?

· WORD FILL 1 ·

Find a three-letter word (which is garden or plant related) that completes each trio of longer words.

1. COM _ _ _ E / DES _ _ _ IC / A_ _ _ HECARY

2. C _ _ _ PER / ORT _ _ _ AEDIC / C _ _ _ STICKS

3. IM _ _ _ CH / S _ _ _ KER / AP _ _ _ SE

4. GLU _ _ _ E / VIS _ _ _ ITY / NAR _ _ _ IS

5. DIMI _ _ _ IVE / MI _ _ _ E / U _ _ _ TERABLE

· ENRICHMENT ·

A number of solutions are, or could provide, 1 Across.

Across

1. Reinvigorate sterile fir with this soil enhancer? (10)

9. Rambling rose on herbarium initially, is towards the land (7)

10. Perhaps setter grew *Rosa canina* (3,4)

11. Monk's head leads all beneficent brethren of town (5)

12. Erroneously taunt Hugo with a proverbially difficult problem (1,5,3)

14 and 7 Down. Protector against the rain surrounds supporter with klaxon – it's all potential 1 Across! (4,3,4)

16. Small drink may produce a mottled effect (7)

18. See 1 Down

20. Telecom posting holds 1 Across? (7)

22. Metal is wryly amusing me (9)

24. Without right fruit, it's wide open (5)

25. Kitchen or bedroom furniture? (7)

27. Come back to one's senses about a vigil (7)

28. Broaden icy arrangement to provide string of 1s and 0s (6,4)

Down

1 and 18 Across. 1 Across that foolish bod banned mistakenly (4,5,3,4)

2. Decay covers large perch (5)

3. Country deer follow one with rut initially (7)

4. Inside take the edges off window, and worse! (7)

5. Beggar clutches foodstuff (3)

6. 1 Across available at shop bizarrely (6)

7. See 14 Across

8. Settle with initial change of direction – this could sting (6)

13. Writer of fairy tales is gloomy we hear (5)

15. Poem follows sailor home (5)

17. Soft cap perhaps tucked inside soft stockings may provide 1 Across (9)

18. Initially, a Royal Marine anti- submarine destroyer attacks a large fleet (6)

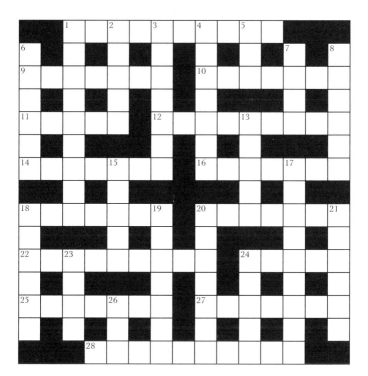

19. In this African country, peculiar rite is seen in time (7)
20. 1 Across may audibly break loose (7)
21. Sat back and set up samples (6)
23. Close perhaps audible in Scottish valley (4)

24. 1 Across discovered in the heart of iguanodon (5)
26. Amid red-skinned onions is a runner? (3)

· COMMON OR GARDEN ·

Give the common name for each of the following:

1. *Philadelphus coronarius*

2. *Hedera helix*

3. *Kniphofia*

4. *Nepeta*

5. *Eschscholzia*

6. *Alcea rosea*

7. *Veronica*

8. *Persicaria*

9. *Lonicera*

10. *Iberis*

11. *Papaver*

12. *Echinops*

13. *Digitalis*

14. *Freesia*

15. *Vicia faba*

16. *Osteospermum*

17. *Hyacinthoides non-scripta*

18. *Dianthus*

19. *Aesculus hippocastanum*

20. *Nigella damascena*

Give the scientific name for each of the following:

1. Snowdrop	11. Snapdragon
2. Grape hyacinth	12. St John's wort
3. Montbretia	13. Busy lizzie
4. Tobacco plant	14. Wallflower
5. Rose	15. Sage
6. Marigold	16. Sweet pea
7. Baby's breath	17. Lavender
8. Thyme	18. Forget-me-not
9. Viburnum	19. Sweet woodruff
10. Coneflower	20. Butterfly bush

· FRUITY FAVOURITES ·

The names of 18 types of fruit are hidden in the grid. As you find
them and cross them off, list them in the spaces below the grid.

E	O	T	N	I	E	M	J	Z	V	U	F	L	E	P
T	O	N	N	L	E	M	I	L	A	E	A	F	T	L
D	L	L	P	A	P	R	I	C	O	T	C	K	A	U
B	A	P	S	J	R	N	D	J	Y	Q	H	H	N	M
K	A	M	V	Q	O	R	S	R	U	X	E	C	A	M
V	Q	F	S	P	H	P	U	I	K	H	R	A	R	I
A	T	O	E	O	W	A	N	C	Y	R	R	E	G	D
G	R	A	P	E	N	C	N	R	K	K	Y	P	E	F
X	R	P	U	M	E	G	R	A	P	C	P	W	M	G
Y	X	Q	C	N	E	E	O	Q	N	M	A	P	O	I
E	V	B	M	W	B	L	X	S	D	A	F	L	P	F
E	E	Y	I	P	J	H	O	A	I	F	B	M	B	M
X	S	Q	S	L	F	K	X	N	S	B	X	H	D	I
U	W	A	E	G	N	A	R	O	Z	M	R	R	R	N
L	R	R	S	G	Z	F	Y	L	X	E	Z	Q	Q	D

——————— ——————— ——————— ———————

——————— ——————— ——————— ———————

——————— ——————— ———————

——————— ——————— ———————

· WORD LADDER 2 ·

H	O	P	S
1			
2			
3			
4			
B	E	E	R

Change the word from HOPS to BEER. Change one letter each time, so that each step forms a new word.

· TOPIARY ANAGRAMS ·

A CUE RESTS _____

FORCE IN _____

RUNG PIN _____

LO! BIKES _____

HIND EGG _____

DO BOW, OX _____

MAY DRIP _____

RASHES _____

· POETIC GARDEN ·

All clues contain a rhyme but are otherwise straightforward.

Across

5. Its sweet-scented trail to please willnot fail (11)

7. White-feathered and grand on lake or on land (4)

8. Small, hot and sweet, in salads they're neat (8)

9. Royal Ordnance ground? A boy by the sound (6)

10. Can be eaten this means, like cabbage or beans (6)

12. Willows are these – the same kind of trees (6)

14. Soil fertile enough? Then you won't need this stuff (6)

15. Tree with smooth bark and not very dark (8)

17. A fence part or bird – the same little word (4)

18. Can be done to roads or drive, as it helps them to survive (11)

Down

1. Overwhelm by flood, or mail could be good (8)

2. Strong kind of seed: an unlikely breed (6)

3. A very small pool as a general rule (6)

4. Used in the snow, going downhill, you know (4)

5. Mary, Mary, quite contrary, _ _ _ garden grow? (3,4,4)

6. Bloom that keeps so very well; also known as *immortelle* (11)

11. How to make a sweet bouquet of blended colours and array (8)

13. Hand tool that you sometimes use if your mower's blown a fuse (6)

14. Kind of grass that's grand and tall; it can show above the wall (6)

16. Home for birds and also ants. Don't get the latter in your pants! (4)

27

· TV AND RADIO ·

1. Who were the two friends of Little Weed in the children's television show set in a garden, first broadcast in 1952?

2. Which garden did Dan Pearson spend 'a year at' for a television series?

3. What was the original title of the BBC radio show now known as *Gardeners' Question Time*?

4. TV gardening show *Ground Force* was hosted by Alan Titchmarsh, Charlie Dimmock and who else?

5. What was the surname of Tom and Barbara, the gardeners who tried to be self-sufficient in a popular 1970s British sitcom?

6. When *Gardeners' Question Time* panellist Bill Sowerbutts appeared on *Desert Island Discs* in 1973, what kind of seeds did he request as his luxury item?
   a) Tobacco
   b) Carrot
   c) Wild flowers
   d) Runner bean

7. What was the name of the gardener in the children's TV programme *The Herbs*?

8. In 2011, *Gardeners' Question Time* made a 'guest appearance' on another Radio 4 programme. What was it?

9. Name one of the 'Curious Gardeners'.

10. In 2008, Monty Don went '*Around the World in …*' what?

11. Name one of the two long-running *Gardeners' Question Time* panellists with appropriately garden-related surnames.

12. What is the name of the British television series featuring two ladies with herbal names who are gardeners and amateur detectives?

13. Which of these locations has hosted *Gardeners' Question Time*?
    a) A prison
    b) A London underground station
    c) A naturist camp
    d) A zoo

14. Alan Titchmarsh began his television career with appearances as the 'horticulture expert' on which long-running magazine programme?

15. What is the name of Monty Don's golden retriever, who inspired a book?

16. True or false? The topic that generates the most questions on *Gardeners' Question Time* is how to make good compost.

17. Which early presenter of *Gardeners' World* presented the show from his garden 'The Magnolias' near Shrewsbury?

18. Which house and garden in Cheshire was used as the setting for the BBC's adaptation of *Pride and Prejudice?*

19. Who was Laurence Llewellyn-Bowen's co-presenter on *Home Front?*

20. Which early 'celebrity gardener' appeared on television with both Morecambe & Wise and Benny Hill?

· IN THE PINK ·

```
I A I D U C A H N T U F G N E
I Z S L T Y Y R K A E U O R V
K A W P I N K C E K D I P C O
X L R L J O P A L T T P S A L
P E N S T E M O N A A I L M G
F A N E O P E H N G M V K E X
G U S J Y U Y R X K I E A L O
I O C H F A A M Y O T Q N L F
R P P H C C U Y P P O P Z I P
C L I I S I T A M E L C H A L
M X N L N I L E E N H W T B G
M T S A U L A X S F J R D V B
H C R S I T T N J F V W W R Y
I E E U R A S T I L B E K W F
G S M U J V U E Q G J G F G L
```

Poppy	Rose	Clematis	Foxglove
Carnation	Azalea	Astilbe	Allium
Tulip	Camellia	Fuchsia	Geranium
Peony	Hyacinth	Penstemon	
Cyclamen	Pink	Lavatera	

· PLUS ONE 2 ·

Each answer is an anagram of the one above, with one letter added. The final, unclued, answer is a plant, flower or shrub.

Popular hot drink

Tidy

Envoy or representative

Consuming

· WORDFLOWER 2 ·

Using the letters in the flower, make as many words as you can of four or more letters. Each word must use the letter in the centre and no letter can be used more times than it appears in the flower. Use all nine letters to make the name of a flower or plant.

Goal:
a minimum of 25 words.

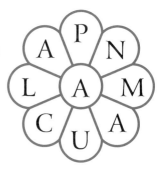

9-letter word

– – – – – – – – –

· CAPABILITY BROWN ·

Eleven answers are associated with landscape gardening.

Across

1. People can walk on this in camp at Harrogate (4)
3. See 10
6. First of all buy expensive new cushions, handmade, for garden seat (5)
10. and 3 It can hold back earth, walling near it being demolished (9,4)
11. Kind of barrier found in defences (5)
12. Hormone, from islets named somewhat unusually 'Langerhans', is neutral first of all (7)
13. Quits after middle of ice splits (7)
14. Level area below garden last of all, for groomed grass (4)
16. Astute variation for this effigy (6)
18. Land suitable for a snooze? (3)
21. However, many are prudent last of all (3)
22. Admit to holy orders unruly first two-thirds of ordinands (6)
23. Puts to some purpose 50% of crocuses (4)
25. Mother and father aren't included in political survey initially (7)
27. Around beginning of ramp create revised raised paved area (7)
29. Initially the Italian aristocracy revered any richly jewelled head ornament worn by women (5)
30. So, Len made mixed drinks (9)
31. Some boyo ate naan made of oatmeal (5)
32. It could have roses growing over it in Ongar church (4)
33. Where ducks may be found in coop on Dartmoor (4)

Down

1. Trial play revised? Not completely (9)
2. Carries young children around crèche finally (5)
4. Estranged being from outer space consumed dinner at first (9)
5. Part of blog I concocted is sound reasoning (5)
6. Self-service meal little Edward battered (8)
7. First bit of news: note Sven reorganised insignificant occasions (3-6)
8. Takes notice of seed scattered after end of March (5)
9. Blooming instrument? (5)

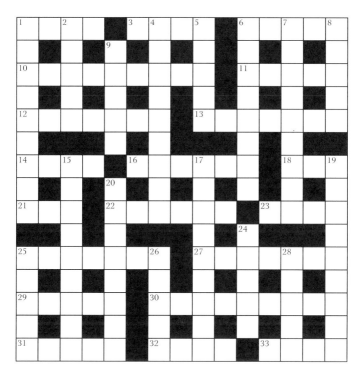

15. Carry transparent colourless liquid in front: it can be used in street cleaning (5,4)

17. Part of stria, Tom, I collected, consisting of three atoms (9)

19. Presided awkwardly consuming Society's first spread (9)

20. It spouts water into a fun swirl (8)

24. Things can be stored in this part of a tree (5)

25. A pot I revamped for this garden area (5)

26. Some rehearsals ameliorated Latin-American dance (5)

28. Car manufacturer adds the ultimate in stereo sound (5)

· GARDEN A–Z ·

The answers are in alphabetical order.

1. This plant is an A–Z of its own, with the Latin name of *Zantedeschia aethiopica* and which common name?

2. By what other name is the Himalayan Poppy known?

3. What is the botanical name of the beauty berry shrub, which produces distinctive violet-coloured berries?

4. Which deciduous shrub is grown as much for the colour of its stems when the leaves have fallen, as for its foliage and flowers?

5. What are *Bergenias* more commonly known as?

6. Which perennial herb has yellow flowers, feathery leaves and a distinctive aniseed flavour?

7. Which spice, related to turmeric and cardamom, is often used in sweet as well as savoury recipes?

8. Which nuts are also known as cobnuts?

9. This flower can be, amongst other things, 'stinking' or 'bearded'. What is it?

10. 'When the bloom of the --- tree is here, Christmas time is near.' To which tree does this Australian song refer?

11. What is the name of the bulbous brassica sometimes nicknamed the 'turnip cabbage'?

12. Which native British tree has leaves that are a favourite with caterpillars and blossom that was used in the past to make a soothing tea?

13. Which evergreen shrub with small yellow flowers gives off a strong, sweet scent in mid winter?

14. Which spice is native to Indonesia and at one time was so valuable that just a small amount could make your fortune?

15. Which exotic flowering plants are mainly epiphytic (grow on trees) or lithophytic (grow on rocks)?

16. What term is used to describe plants that live for more than two years, and stay in the ground all year round?

17. Which evergreen plant (genus *Briza*) takes its common name from the way it moves in the breeze?

18. Which easy-to-grow summer salad vegetable has varieties that include Ping Pong and Sparkler?

19. Which conifer is known for the strength of its wood, and is often used to make telegraph poles?

20. Which spice is a staple of Asian recipes, can be used as a dye, and has a reputation for aiding in arthritic conditions?

21. What is the scientific name for the spiny shrub known as gorse or furze?

22. What term is used to describe leaves that are more than one colour?

23. Who was the 18th-century scientist and botanist after whom a genus of plants in the iris family is named?

24. What is the name for the vessels in plants used to transport water from the roots to the leaves?

25. Of which type of tree can Britain boast ten examples that predate the 10th century?

26. Which colourful annual is easy to grow from seed and shares its name with a Pokémon character?

· IN THE SHED ·

The names of 18 things that you might find in the garden shed are hidden in the grid. As you find them and cross them off, list them in the spaces below the grid.

U	F	V	N	O	E	J	A	G	V	S	M	T	T	S
T	H	O	S	E	P	U	R	U	I	S	N	S	W	B
X	R	V	Z	I	Q	P	E	L	E	N	X	O	I	L
R	W	O	R	R	A	B	L	E	E	H	W	P	N	U
K	E	C	W	S	O	E	D	G	U	R	T	M	E	B
E	Z	S	U	E	R	S	S	R	Q	G	F	O	S	A
S	D	L	I	T	L	P	X	U	G	I	L	C	E	I
L	K	A	N	L	S	H	E	A	R	S	R	I	A	I
P	E	X	P	R	I	L	J	S	E	M	P	U	Z	C
W	O	O	E	S	J	T	S	B	P	I	R	O	R	H
L	N	Q	H	L	V	D	R	X	P	E	T	A	T	F
F	D	T	D	T	R	U	C	E	W	W	K	M	C	S
O	I	C	I	I	P	S	N	O	F	E	P	K	Q	W
R	R	G	E	P	S	O	M	W	C	W	N	F	E	P
K	R	V	F	X	Y	Z	E	S	E	N	A	C	U	X

_____   _____   _____   _____

_____   _____   _____   _____

_____   _____   _____   _____

_____   _____   _____

· CABBAGE COUNTING ·

On his allotment, Bert has 10 cabbages, three times as many leeks, and half as many tomato plants as leeks. If we call the tomatoes cabbages, how many cabbages will he have?

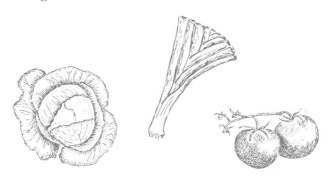

· WORD FILL 2 ·

Find a three-letter word (which is garden or plant related) that completes each trio of longer words.

1. D _ _ _ R / YESTE _ _ _ AR / F _ _ _ RS

2. MI _ _ _ PLY / SOU _ _ _ HONE / DI _ _ _ POINT

3. G _ _ _ HERD / L _ _ _ HE / FL _ _ _ ING

4. HY _ _ _ ERMIC / CHIRO _ _ _ Y / ANTI _ _ _ ES

5. GN _ _ _ ED / W _ _ _ ABLE / FL _ _ _ BACK

· A THORNY PROBLEM ·

The ten clues in italics (which have no definition) yield an
answer which is the name of a plant or genus which can be
a problem to handle as it has thorns, spikes or prickles.

Across

1. Percolate underlying surface in part of sewage works (6,3)
6. and 11. *Meet loner, all mixed up* (5,4)
9. It could be a nuclear one concerning person in film (7)
10. *Resort in Omaha* (7)
11. See 6
12. Stagger back from heartless collier, upset (6)
14. Chemical substance found in cooling ash (3)
16. Leave behind pi tutors in disarray (8)
17. A police department I contacted initially is sharp (6)
20. Considerate Penny keeps back plant that attracts cats (6)
22. *What changed in brass instrument?* (8)
25. Conifer found in Glengariff, Ireland (3)
26. *Odd bits of confit course* (6)
27. *Refer to this clue last of all* (4)
29. *Flat bottomed boat surrounded by leaders of oriental indigenous army* (7)
31. Offer to continue resistance (4,3)
32. *Girl who may be rather prickly* (5)
33. Sioux in disarray following order banning new occupancies initially

Down

1. *Rhine fort demolished* (9)
2. Thinnest home for a bird at end of meadow (7)
3. Devours some neat sandwiches (4)
4. *Sort first of black berries* (8)
5. Nomad returns around first of September for fruit (6)
6. Note part of axilla hurts (3)
7. Male, advanced in years, coped (7)
8. Gets close to Newcastle, expecting awfully rutted snow first of all (5)
13. Find half of Polo feline espied initially (6)
15. Atmospheric disturbances in radio reception in disorganised attics (6)

18. Musical compositions
and musical events about
nothing! (9)

19. Monkey put broken chain
round cup upside down (8)

21. An act of chasing upset
Ursula after perspiring
initially (7)

23. Four circular letters included,
at intervals, full colour
adverts last of all, for sherry
(7)

24. Mike mostly has trouble in
Gilbert and Sullivan opera
(6)

25. Decay in fruit harvest
initially produces a mass of
small bubbles (5)

28. *Some useful example* (4)

30. Attempt a means of scoring
in rugby (3)

· LITERARY LINKS ·

1. Which fruit did the owl and the pussycat eat with a runcible spoon?

2. Which John le Carré novel explores corruption in the pharmaceutical industry?

3. Which terrifying plants were created by John Wyndham in 1951?

4. Name one of the two characters in *The Forsyte Saga* who had plant-related names.

5. In *Hamlet*, when Ophelia hands out flowers and herbs, what does she say 'is for remembrance'?

6. Sukebind, a fictional plant with aphrodisiac properties, appeared in which 1932 novel?

7. In which series of books would you come across the Whomping Willow?

8. Which novel by Ernest Hemingway was published posthumously in 1986?

9. Which flower is central to John McCrae's poem 'In Flanders Fields'?

10. In *Through the Looking Glass*, Alice finds herself in the Garden of Live Flowers. Name two of the flowers that talk to her.

11. Which Hans Christian Andersen fairy tale features a vegetable in its title?

12. In the book by Antoine de Saint-Exupéry, which tree does the Little Prince fear in case it takes over his asteroid?

13. Who penned the line 'Come into the garden, Maud' in a poem of 1855?

14. Which grain features in the title of a 1951 novel by J.D. Salinger?

15. In which enduringly popular children's book does a young boy find himself in another place and time when the clock strikes thirteen?

16. Which Shakespearean character laments the plight of Denmark by describing it as 'an unweeded garden / That grows to seed'?

17. Which Virginia Woof short story shares its name with a famous botanical garden?

18. In which Dickens novel is a character surprised, and at the same time strangely flattered, when her neighbour starts throwing cucumbers over her garden wall?

19. In which book do the 'blood-red rhododendrons' remind the narrator of her husband's first wife?

20. In Philip Pullman's *His Dark Materials* trilogy, what is the location for the annual midsummer 'reunion' of Lyra and Will, even though they inhabit separate parallel worlds?

· GARDEN FRIENDS AND FOES ·

E	B	H	S	S	J	N	U	F	A	I	L	K	K	I
Y	A	A	O	T	B	T	O	O	R	A	G	F	H	N
L	Z	R	T	R	T	C	F	T	C	A	O	D	I	M
F	U	B	T	Y	N	P	D	E	X	K	X	G	P	N
R	E	U	V	H	B	E	W	M	O	L	E	V	P	T
E	B	T	Z	C	W	I	T	U	L	M	U	G	S	L
V	Z	T	S	O	N	O	G	O	H	E	G	D	E	H
O	D	E	W	G	J	W	R	F	S	O	M	R	M	P
H	C	R	B	C	P	T	J	M	M	R	R	B	O	S
G	W	F	I	S	P	I	D	E	R	I	F	E	U	A
U	A	L	M	B	S	S	F	F	U	G	A	E	S	W
W	P	Y	G	Z	Y	Y	D	Q	R	P	U	E	E	D
C	G	O	O	F	T	D	S	Y	H	Q	R	L	O	I
K	R	X	J	N	Y	A	A	I	X	K	J	C	S	D
F	Q	Y	J	H	M	U	D	L	I	A	N	S	B	W

Lacewing	Slug	Bee	Mole
Earthworm	Aphid	Hornet	Hoverfly
Bat	Wasp	Frog	Squirrel
Spider	Hedgehog	Ladybird	
Mouse	Butterfly	Snail	

42

· WORD LADDER 3 ·

L	E	A	F
1			
2			
3			
4			
S	T	E	M

Change the word from LEAF to STEM. Change one letter each time, so that each step forms a new word.

· UNDERGROUND ANAGRAMS ·

DO REHASH, SIR! _____
HI LO BARK _____
BOOT TREE _____
KOREA ITCH _____
PAN RIPS _____
RACE LICE _____
CURE IT, MR! _____
OAT TOP _____

· PLANT CROSSING ·

Across clues refer to plants or the product of plants.

Across

1. Honeydew or 11 Across (4,5)
6. A tropical fruit with pink juicy flesh (5)
9. Tree of the Mulberry family (5)
10. A pea with edible pod (9)
11. Small round fruit with orange flesh (10)
12. Edible seed from leguminous plant (4)
14. Common edible green 12 (3,4)
15. Snapdragon relation with colourful funnel-shaped flowers (7)
17. Possibly a rose on walkabout (7)
19. Tree and nut possibly Hazel or Cob (7)
20. Fruit of beech, oak or chestnut – pigs love them (4)
22. Fast-growing evergreen Australasian tree valued for its wood, oil, gum, and resin (10)
25. Flowery weed that sounds like a foppish cat (9)
26. Nut might be chewed for stimulation (5)
27. Cabbage family often found in 23 Down (5)
28. Of the daisy family with tall spikes of small bright yellow flowers (9)

Down

1. A thousand and one, a thousand and one hundred – take off! (5)
2. Use force with powerful weapon (6-3)
3. Sky mail network used in error (10)
4. Ridicule light opera premiere – no going back (7)
5. After one over the eight, Peg found in alley (7)
6. Actress sounding close to endless depression . . . (4)
7. . . . on a high in rehab, overacts (5)
8. In seat at ten, Dan tips waiter (9)
13. Space manoeuvre can, and does prove to be useful (10)
14. As a first aider, I get in a cramped position (9)
16. He watches Prescott and ACAS leader fall out (9)
18. Exciting ruins go to be rebuilt (7)

19. Soft soap for washing face? (7)
21. Char to air before closing house (5)
23. Caesar served at table, might need dressing . . . (5)
24. . . . for dining room in a terrible state (4)

· FOOD AND DRINK ·

1. Which berry is used to give gin its distinctive flavour?

2. What is a shaddock?

3. Which pulse is used to make hummus?

4. Both the fruit and flowers of British plant *Sambucus* can be made into wine. What is its common name?

5. Which fruit features in the dessert named for Dame Nellie Melba, the opera singer?

6. True or false? The Irish drink poteen (or poitín) is named after the potatoes from which it is distilled.

7. Which fruit flavours the cordial used in Kir Royale?

8. What is the principal ingredient in guacamole?

9. What was the name of the Second World War initiative that encouraged people to grow their own food?

10. In which tropical fruit would you find the natural digestive aid papain?

11. Which part of the cardoon plant would you eat?

12. Which grain is used to make semolina?

13. In the children's nursery rhyme, what grew on 'my little nut-tree'?

14. Which part of the vanilla orchid is dried for use as a culinary flavouring?

15. Which fruit is used to make the French spirit Calvados?

16. What is the main vegetable ingredient in moussaka?

17. Of which family is endive a member?

18. Cider is made from apples. What is the name of the similar drink made from pears?

19. In the stories of Persephone in Greek mythology, what is said to be the fruit of the underworld?

20. What was the first vegetable grown in space?

· HARVEST TIME ·

18 words that relate to the season of harvesting are hidden in the grid. As you find them and cross them off, list them in the spaces below the grid.

T	I	U	R	F	U	S	H	J	R	G	M	L	N	J
I	V	H	J	Q	D	T	A	W	L	E	A	Z	R	P
N	M	U	T	U	A	O	R	I	R	V	H	E	O	R
D	K	I	U	F	Q	R	V	O	I	R	P	T	C	I
D	L	P	E	C	G	E	E	T	M	I	E	N	A	A
C	R	E	B	O	E	M	S	V	R	U	E	E	Y	G
E	M	S	I	C	S	E	T	W	A	G	H	Y	B	D
L	S	B	H	Y	F	K	G	J	S	T	H	L	H	R
K	U	R	M	E	O	B	U	R	Y	Q	B	B	E	X
C	P	I	C	K	A	M	L	C	A	R	Z	A	O	C
I	E	Q	S	P	P	V	S	B	Q	I	P	M	R	H
S	F	T	U	T	Q	E	E	P	I	I	N	O	M	J
P	R	E	S	E	R	V	E	S	N	E	P	F	A	F
W	H	E	A	T	M	B	P	G	S	K	J	O	D
P	P	T	H	I	D	Y	M	V	V	S	T	M	O	O

_____ _____ _____

_____ _____ _____

_____ _____ _____

_____ _____ _____

· PLUS ONE 3 ·

Each answer is an anagram of the one above, with one letter added. The final, unclued, answer is a plant, flower or shrub.

Period of history

Genuine

Before the expected time

Conference or negotiation

· WORDFLOWER 3 ·

Using the letters in the flower, make as many words as you can of four or more letters. Each word must use the letter in the centre and no letter can be used more times than it appears in the flower. Use all nine letters to make the name of a garden visitor.

Goal:
a minimum of 20 words.

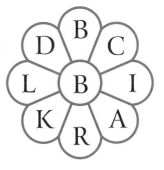

9-letter word

_ _ _ _ _ _ _ _ _

· POT POURRI ·

Across

1. They dig the garden or get their cards? (6)
5. Pin on board those things that grieve gardeners (6)
10. Perennials planted in a bed is right by Uncle Sam . . . (7)
11. . . . in Lincoln: good chap, the Italian, for perennials (7)
12. Coneflower plants die back; it's tricky east of Rugby (9)
13. Hollyhocks left by church temperance types coming round (5)
14. Herb – an Open follower? (6)
16. Their leaves are spent covering Eve's blushes? (3,5)
19. Spanish broom's pole one can jab into guts (8)
20. Half garden, half lichen plant (6)
22. Rotten matter of Lisa being banned from a dodgy music hall (5)
24. Girl rejected number in obsession for foxglove-type flowers (9)
27. 22 get mail after head of clan's order (7)
28. Thrift of a marine rose (3,4)
29. American deserted the Big Apple completely, going back to the artichokes (6)
30. A half-ridiculous pasture flower (6)

Down

2. St Bruno's Lily is in exhibition on the first of August (9)
3. Hundred rupees is, in part, to provide fruit with a single seed (5)
4. In the van, slim tall and lissom Kniphofia make up the floral section (5)
5. The Harlequin flower is a shop line (8)
6. Sinatra at jazz is a true perennial (9)
7. Plant's one to protect in a fall of hail (5)
8. Like hard skin in fruit of the oak (6)
9. They have branches in Lebanon? (6)
15. Alamo hit badly: about time to take stock (9)
17. Insect's cut mark, for example, seen on the head of a rose (9)

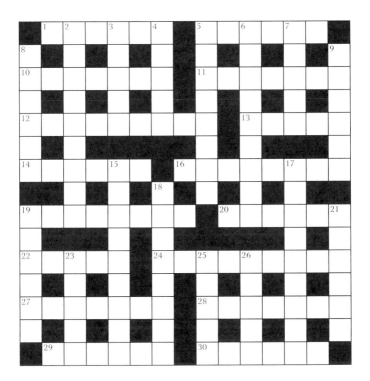

18. Loosely tie support around goldtopped evergreen (8)

19. Quantity found on a church of the Rhus genus (6)

21. Something used on board over years of low acidity (6)

23. Yank slight Royal Navy man to get close to 21 (5)

25. Put on the station house plantain lilies (5)

26. Integrifolia named after one of the Phillipses (5)

· GENERAL KNOWLEDGE 2 ·

1. What is a 'blind' plant?

2. What is another name for the rowan tree?

3. In Norse mythology, what kind of tree is Yggdrasil, the tree of life?

4. What is tilth?

5. Where would you find 'Potato Eaters'?
   a) In your vegetable patch
   b) On a bookshelf
   c) In a gallery
   d) In an aviary

6. To which continent is teak native?

7. What would you be doing if you were in Scotland 'tattie howking'?

8. Which laundry product was at one time made from the juice of bluebell bulbs?

9. The 'berries' of *Pyracantha* are scientifically known as what?

10. Larkspur is the common name for which genus of flowering plants?

11. Which garden pest goes by the Latin name of *Talpa europaea*?

12. In gardening terms, what is a 'maiden'?

13. With what would you fill a French drain?

14. Which part of a tree is used to make corks?

15. What type of leaves does a 'hirsute' plant have?

16. Which fruit links Earl Grey tea and Eau de Cologne?

17. What is the common name of *Acer rubrum*?

18. Which vegetable did Mark Twain describe as 'Cabbage with a college education'?

19. Which fungal infection causes pustules on the underside of brassica leaves?

20. Why is it necessary to be wary of *Berberis* plants?
    a) They are poisonous
    b) They are thorny
    c) They attract wasps
    d) The foliage can irritate the skin

· APPLES & PEARS ·

```
Y N P M L G D K A E N D Y B E
I Y R I O I C I L H V I R S M
R I E L P O F L S H Q A N J P
A H D L N P E I T C E D O Q I
Z E L N M N I E L B O A N N R
N M A Q O A B N U N R V C A E
S C Y G Z V R R O R N J E T X
I R R R N M N B P E Y O N R D
U A W O L G N O O M M N E A Y
J H O N E Y C R I S P A U P X
M A H R O G G A L A F G C S Y
U G I H S T F S M S S O G D C
X C N J A E E A J D K L E Q P
R U S S E T U F H M R D A O W
G H F X M A A W R K D V A Y Z
```

Zari	Gala	Pippin	Gorham
Beth	Russet	Empire	Discovery
Bramley	Jargonelle	Golden	Moonglow
Jonagold	Cameo	Honeycrisp	
Spartan	Cannock	Braeburn	

· WATER WOES ·

Sue needs exactly four pints of water to dilute some fertiliser. She has a three-pint watering can and a five-pint watering can. How can she use these to measure the amount that she needs?

· WORD FILL 3 ·

Find a three-letter word (which is garden or plant related) that completes each trio of longer words.

1. SUB _ _ _ LE / FIC _ _ _ IOUS / DES _ _ _ UTE

2. GUN _ _ _ HTER / DIS _ _ _ URED / CON _ _ _ URE

3. S _ _ _ AN / APO _ _ _ Y / THEO _ _ _ Y

4. PARA _ _ _ M / PE _ _ _ REE / IN _ _ _ NANT

5. S _ _ _ ED / CR _ _ _ Y / CL _ _ _ ROOM

· A-Mazing ·

The last letter of each answer is the first letter of the next answer. All answers are flowers and are clued as anagrams.

1. canal puma
2. shut a pagan
3. user flown
4. Don horned Rod
5. nail leg
6. such a tan
7. rows pond
8. mop riser
9. inelegant
10. Elise weds
11. no grandpas
12. suit nut arm
13. Wade mows tee
14. the list
15. I care
16. a don's roar
17. I lined hump
18. main goal
19. Mary is all
20. welds peel
21. I steer fools

· WHEN IS A GARDEN NOT A GARDEN? ·

'Garden' features in every answer, but not all are the kind that you can grow plants in.

1. What is the nickname for the US state of New Jersey?

2. The Beatles sang, 'I'd like to be under the sea…' – where?

3. Which garden was home to Adam and Eve?

4. What is the name of the 17th-century apothecary's garden that can still be visited today in Hospital Road, London?

5. Who is the well-known comedian and broadcaster who created *I'm Sorry I Haven't A Clue*?

6. Which garden in literature was restored by a little girl who came to England from India?

7. Which phrase means 'the usual or familiar type'?

8. Which World War II military operation took place in the Netherlands in September 1944?

9. Which London district features, amongst other things, a market and an opera house?

10. Where would you find Makka Pakka and Upsy Daisy?

11. What is the colloquial term for a period of extended paid leave from work?

12. What is the name of the famous triptych painted by artist Hieronymus Bosch in the 16th century, depicting themes including sinful pleasure and hellish punishment?

13. What is the name of the public park in Colorado Springs, USA, originally known as Red Rock Corral?

14. By what name is the English county of Kent sometimes known?

15. What is the name of the famous arena in Manhattan, known for hosting huge sporting and musical events?

16. Name one of the two towns in Hertfordshire created in the early 20th century on the principles of Ebenezer Howard.

17. Which garden did Siouxsie and the Banshees sing about?

18. Which street, and district, in London is famous as the jewellery quarter?

19. Which Australian pop duo had several UK hits in the late 1990s and early 2000s?

20. What is the name of the 300-km stretch of South African coast, renowned for its beauty and diverse variety of vegetation and landscapes?

· STARTING FROM SCRATCH ·

*Hidden in the grid are 18 things that you might need to create a new
garden. As you find them and cross them off, list them in the spaces
below the grid.*

S	A	G	S	K	C	I	R	B	E	T	S	U	H	G
M	G	F	R	U	T	P	E	N	Q	E	T	Q	M	N
R	E	N	L	A	L	R	T	J	Q	X	D	R	B	I
V	A	C	I	A	V	H	E	D	G	I	N	G	T	C
S	Y	T	N	T	U	E	R	O	C	D	R	A	H	N
X	E	T	R	S	T	L	L	M	Y	S	V	B	F	E
G	S	E	I	O	I	U	Y	E	B	J	N	U	G	F
D	H	A	D	O	M	P	C	A	S	W	C	L	C	D
L	S	T	S	S	F	Z	L	A	N	B	V	B	S	Z
M	A	P	J	Z	E	S	N	T	E	P	Y	S	Q	C
O	O	P	L	N	D	D	Z	G	U	P	G	M	W	Y
T	N	Y	A	D	G	G	D	S	J	Q	R	W	W	C
P	O	S	T	S	I	E	M	U	I	M	E	M	F	C
O	P	H	U	V	N	W	E	E	Y	F	N	M	J	F
B	H	G	W	H	G	G	Z	H	L	X	E	W	J	G

_____ _____ _____ _____

_____ _____ _____ _____

_____ _____ _____ _____

_____ _____ _____

_____ _____ _____

· WORD LADDER 4 ·

V	I	N	E
1			
2			
3			
4			
5			
B	U	S	H

Change the word from VINE to BUSH. Change one letter each time, so that each step forms a new word.

· SALAD ANAGRAMS ·

A CREW RESTS _____

BEG RICE _____

ACID CHOIR _____

NO IRE, MA! _____

CAN SHIP _____

A BURNT POSSE _____

ORCA EELS _____

A RED HISS _____

· CLIMBING FRUIT ·

All the Across clues are normal. The answers to the Down clues are all fruit and therefore these clues have no definitions. The answers to Down clues are entered 'climbing'.

Across

7. Bar foreign nobleman and queen (7)

8. Daring man in East becomes brave lady (7)

10. Small city gets nearly rich on lemon acid (6)

11. Spellers are attractive girls (8)

12. Charts go back to wartime meat (4)

13. Eli changes in repose (3)

14. Son has hatred for metallic element (6)

15. Gem weight (5)

17. Finally glutinous jam became a lesser sticky mark (5)

22. Tool for smoothing wood sounds less pretty (6)

24. To start with Peter is eating tart (3)

26. Defeat with crouton – it's no trick! (4)

27. Note to remember concerning babysitter (8)

28. Inn too unsettled for idea (6)

29. Tree holding upper class is in (7)

30. Characteristic gold for one who commits treason (7)

Down

1. It's hot in a Capri cottage in the summer (7)

2. Crossing the Tamar in dinghy can be dangerous (8)

3. Some of his remarks are really cheeky (6)

4. Jonah Lomu's cat elected to sleep on his bed (8)

5. At first Adam's only man in Eden (6)

6. When I heard the noise recur ran to mother immediately (7)

9. Having eaten a canape a child is sick (5)

16. Command a ring of riot police (8)

18. If I am the victor I am going to celebrate (8)

19. A mushroom like the morel loves shady woodland (7)

20. When you visit Agra people eat curry (5)

21. In Acapulco con uttered the words that gave him away (7)

23. By discovering old Ur I and my wife gained fame (6)

25. The man playing Captain Corcoran gets several words wrong (6)

· WEATHER LORE ·

1. According to tradition, if March 'comes in like a lion', how will it go out?

2. Complete this well-known weather saying: 'Rain before seven…'

3. 'Mackerel sky, mackerel sky, Never long wet, never long dry.' What kind of clouds make up a mackerel sky?

4. Which old saying refers to the blooming leaves of the ash and oak to predict the coming summer's rain?

5. Which animals predict the coming of rain, according to the following rhyme? 'When --- gather in a huddle / Tomorrow will have a puddle.'

6. What kind of Easter might you expect, according to weather lore, if you've had a green Christmas?

7. 'When windows won't open, and the salt clogs the shaker / The weather will favour…' Who?

8. 'Ne'er cast a clout till May be out.' This saying can be interpreted as referring to the month of May or to the May tree. But what is a 'clout', and what is the saying actually advising?

9. According to popular belief, what kind of weather might you expect if you see cows lying down in a field?

10. 'The taller the --- in the summer / The deeper the snow in the winter'. What should you be looking at on summer days if you're using this saying to predict the winter weather: grass, wheat, weeds or rushes?

11. Perhaps the best-known of all weather-related sayings is 'Red sky at night,

shepherd's delight'. Why does a red evening sky foretell good weather?

12. During the Groundhog Day ceremony in Punxsutawney, USA, on 2nd February, what is predicted if the groundhog sees his shadow?

13. A halo round the moon is said to be a prediction of unsettled weather. What causes the halo?

14. '--- bring May flowers.' A reassurance that rain has its purpose can be found in this little rhyme. What is the missing phrase?

15. A simple weather forecast can be obtained by looking at a pine cone. If the cone has opened up, is this a good sign or a bad sign?

16. 'If woolly fleeces bestow the heavenly way / Be sure no rain will come today.' What is the scientific name for the 'fair-weather' clouds that look like fluffy sheep?

17. According to tradition, if ladybirds swarm, what kind of weather can you expect?

18. If you see sun shining through your apple trees on Christmas day, what, according to folklore, might you expect by way of a crop in the coming year?

19. Which of the following can be used to calculate air temperature?
   a) The rate at which frogs croak
   b) The frequency with which owls hoot
   c) The speed of a woodpecker's tap
   d) The rate at which crickets chirp

20. If your onion skins grow 'thick and tough', what kind of winter is said to be coming your way?

· NATIONAL TRUST GARDENS AND PARKLANDS ·

```
H C X S U N G P E Y A M M H R
C L I V E D E N E M A Z R V E
J U S W M T U L I H O K M C B
Q Q T P W D R N R L C O R U N
Q M Z O A E W Y H P K O R A O
F O R C T R D H R A M C T C T
F T A S R H W O R C M N I N L
H T O N I A W G I K S O N L E
G I A T O A G P S W T T S U B
U S P U L M V S H O O R K R M
C F A L X U J Y I O W E L X F
B O A E R D D I G D E L K C L
T N A N D O B E Q X E L X I E
E T D A E H R U O T S I W S G
P A C P G E J U W A B K N J P
```

Bodnant	Stourhead	Cragside	Petworth
Mottisfont	Stowe	Dyrham	Dunham
Osterley	Belton	Erddig	Crom
Rowallane	Blickling	Killerton	
Croome	Cliveden	Packwood	

· PLUS ONE 4 ·

*Each answer is an anagram of the one above, with one
letter added. The final, unclued, answer is a plant,
flower or shrub.*

Beer

Bundle

Hold responsible

Form of limestone, often white

· WORDFLOWER 4 ·

*Using the letters in the flower,
make as many words as you
can of four or more letters. Each
word must use the letter in the
centre and no letter can be used
more times than it appears in
the flower. Use all nine letters
to make the name of a flower or
plant.*

*Goal:
a minimum of 27 words.*

9-letter word

– – – – – – – – –

· BOTTLE-IT ·

The answers to all asterisked clues come from the garden
and may end up in a bottle, can or jar in some form.

Across

7. *Makes an excellent Daiquiri but skin can cause slipups (6)

8. Stick to this place on active duty (6)

9. *Lose playing Gin (4)

10. Top player Erica started at nursery (8)

11. Solvent, having one note to spend (7)

13. *Greens could produce smile (5)

15. *Slump resulted in good jobs (5)

17. *Wine from Jersey, perhaps, with Pils to follow up (7)

20. No penalty from dodgy Ref, with sector finally lost (4-4)

21. A prerequisite of new wine (4)

22. *Recycle Centre first removed rubbish and turned to salt perhaps (6)

23. *Pulse found to be fast on the Italian (6)

Down

1. *A girl caught changing bulb (6)

2. *Court day? (4)

3. *Unruly rotter removed from demonstrators creating jams (7)

4. *Green jokes about English leader (5)

5. * Ice hills surprisingly are hot . . . (8)

6. *. . . and the colour of old mountains (6)

12. *Fruit and assortment of meats too (8)

14. *A cherry red 2-litre Romeo convertible (7)

16. *Smelly cheese contains fruit (6)

18. The first six in listing work to impress (6)

19. Given a kiss, beams for the pictures (1-4)

21. *Leaves a fortune (4)

· WEED WOES AND PLANT PROBLEMS ·

1. The Weeds Act of 1959 applies to five 'injurious weeds'. Name one.

2. What is the term for fungal infections which cause seedlings to collapse, often covered in white mould?

3. Which weed can be both friend and foe, making a tasty soup or causing a burning sting?

4. How would you recognise botrytis on your plants?

5. The dandelion is known to have diuretic properties, which may explain its French name. What is this?

6. What is the fungal disease that affects wood and leaves, especially on plum, apple, apricot and cherry trees?

7. From where was Mind-your-own-business introduced?

8. If you saw orange streaks and patches on your leeks, what problem would you be experiencing?

9. Ground elder can be a huge problem, but once dug up, what could you do with the leaves?

10. This fungal infection can be downy or powdery. What is it?

11. Mint can become invasive in a garden. What is the best way to stop it from spreading too much?

12. Which plants are susceptible to halo blight?

13. The Romans believed that weeds would not return if they were uprooted at a certain time. When was this?
a) In the fourth quarter of the moon
b) At sunrise
c) On the longest day of the year
d) At night, by starlight

14. Marsh spot is a disease of peas caused by a lack of which element in the soil?

15. Which form of agricultural weed control was banned by the UK government in 1993?

16. Which pests can be deterred by the use of copper strips?

17. Considered an invasive weed in the garden, this plant bears delicious autumn fruit, but legend says that you should not harvest it after Old Michaelmas Day (10th October). What is it?

18. Which disease, caused by the *Albugo* fungus, and also sometimes called staghead, can affect brassicas?

19. What is the huge non-native plant that can cause the skin to become sensitive to sunlight and can even cause temporary blindness?

20. What is the name of the insect whose grubs can cause extensive damage to cane fruits?

· WATER GARDENS ·

18 words that relate to water features are hidden in the grid. As you find them and cross them off, list them in the spaces below the grid.

T	F	T	Y	R	Y	Y	D	T	I	Q	Z	W	B	W
V	A	B	W	B	E	E	L	L	O	T	N	I	U	X
S	Q	D	L	E	E	T	Y	F	K	H	F	F	L	M
X	I	I	P	W	N	R	L	C	N	W	R	Q	R	O
V	L	A	K	O	T	C	C	I	A	O	O	Y	U	B
Y	D	C	G	N	L	O	N	Z	F	R	G	F	S	O
Q	U	G	F	I	Q	E	J	J	E	C	P	A	H	G
D	V	D	Q	A	T	W	B	P	A	C	O	Z	R	N
P	M	U	P	T	W	I	I	A	G	W	E	M	O	D
P	J	E	I	N	I	B	K	A	L	D	V	R	U	C
K	T	N	Z	U	W	G	V	C	A	T	E	D	Z	J
Y	G	U	J	O	P	O	N	D	N	H	Y	M	N	V
X	I	G	I	F	E	K	S	I	M	Y	W	Q	M	N
G	O	L	D	F	I	S	H	E	D	A	C	S	A	C
U	G	Q	Y	A	H	L	C	W	T	H	H	V	A	P

_____ _____ _____ _____

_____ _____ _____ _____

_____ _____ _____ _____

_____ _____ _____ _____

_____ _____ _____

· An Apple a Day ·

Richard has a basket containing five apples from his prize apple tree. How can he divide them among his five grandchildren so that each one has an apple and one apple stays in the basket?

· Word Fill 4 ·

Find a four-letter word (which is garden or plant related) that completes each trio of longer words.

1. HEA _ _ _ _ SS / DI _ _ _ _ D / WA _ _ _ _ SS

2. P _ _ _ _ CUTE / MO _ _ _ _ LY / NEU _ _ _ _ S

3. RES _ _ _ _ S / DES _ _ _ _ ENT / TRANS _ _ _ _ ER

4. SU _ _ _ _ LY / MO _ _ _ _ SS / S _ _ _ _ TS

5. AM _ _ _ _ ED / BA _ _ _ _ KA / ROSE _ _ _ _ ES

· SHOW GARDENS ·

The Royal Horticultural Society is responsible for a number of gardens (1 Across, 3, 5 and 22 combined with 25) and shows (1 Down combined with 24, 11, 12, 18 Down and 21).

Across

1. *Garden*: Lily 'ead one crushes (4,4)

5. *Garden*: Half of island overwhelmed by returning yew (6)

10. Stricken railmen discover ore (7)

11. *Show*: Participants at many a battle of Stamford Bridge? (7)

12. *Show*: Bewildering to trap tank? (6,4)

13. At least alternate characters found in puppet-box (2,2)

15. Espied a drink served without the rocks? (7)

17. As times change, this haar appears (3,4)

18. Shame tips of gardener seen in sequence (7)

20. Could there possibly be a time for connecting rafters with one of these? (3,4)

22. *Garden*: This flower grew (4)

23. Complementary re-planting of cerea finally with a rice crop (10)

26. One of a set of atoms is nothing before most important experiment initially (7)

27. Within Hoover, useless components might cause excessive wear and tear (7)

28. .EU turf may represent the shape of things to come (6)

29. Initially unpopular baked bean with ten following, is undefeated (8)

Down

1. and 24. *Show*: Found in a Southampton courtroom perhaps? (7,5)

2. Prepare seed cake? (5)

3. *Garden*: Mistake a larch row with redwood initially (6,4)

4. Possibly arum notebook provides pond foliage (7)

6. Pinch ends alternately as covered in frost (4)

7. Tries clip possibly when providing value without discount (4,5)

8. A student may take the old one with an utter defeat (4,3)

9. Cereal in when seeds appear (6)

14. No pay increase from geezer with a few changes (4,6)

16. Vehicle possibly directs after one goes left (9)

18. *Show*: The centre of Redcar differs (7)

19. New rooks perhaps have leader removed – they are relatives? (6)

20. Hat found in eccentric ornamentation (7)

21. *Show*: Found in the contents of the formal vernacular (7)

24. See 1.

25. *Garden*: Heath is low before river (4)

· CONNECTIONS ·

*Find one word that links each of the following. The 'link' may form
part of a word or phrase in either or both answers.*

1. Bacchus and John Steinbeck.

2. A Welsh emblem and a small succulent grown in rockeries or on roofs.

3. A delicious eating apple and a bamboo also known as fish-pole bamboo.

4. A white froth on plants and a wooden wall clock.

5. The queen's youngest child and a potato variety.

6. A variety of *Alyssum* and *Galanthus*.

7. A climbing rose and Lassie.

8. A British truck manufacturer and a conifer.

9. Beer ingredients and a children's pavement game.

10. A plant with a spicy root used in a popular sauce and a large, blood-sucking fly.

11. An exotic flower and a championship racehorse.

12. A garden designer and a somewhat unstable Victorian doctor.

13. A prickly houseplant that blooms late in the year and *Helleborus niger*.

14. A common garden bird and a fictional pirate.

15. A climbing plant known for its red autumn foliage and a small bird known colloquially as the tree mouse.

16. *Eschscholzia* and a song by the Mamas and the Papas.

17. A variety of kale and a Stooge.

18. An artichoke and the WI.

19. The grub of a daddy longlegs and a baked potato.

20. A formal, intricately designed garden and a colloquial reference to getting married.

· THE COTTAGE GARDEN ·

```
A Q R C W Q E K N Q M B Y J B
O Z X O M A C N F I P E R Y B
N O L N S O L S I R P E E R P
C N S A T E T L N B D U C M B
W I Y S V W P Y F W M O L U W
Q G C V B E B D D L S U T B K
D E L P H I N I U M O T L L M
A L Y M O Z B D O N E W V O W
I L P A L B E S E R X V E H C
E A P H L O X S F R B L F R V
L H O G Y N A L U N A P M A C
D C P G H K Y E G A R O B N D
D J K F O X G L O V E K U N A
U Y P I C E X M I L M T Y Q E
B G Y L K P V B S A A Y Q Q D
```

Delphinium	Rose	Foxglove	Columbine
Lupin	Campanula	Phlox	Nigella
Hollyhock	Poppy	Cosmos	Wallflower
Bee	Buddleia	Borage	
Butterfly	Stock	Lavender	

· WORD LADDER 5 ·

G	R	A	S	S
1				
2				
3				
4				
5				
L	A	W	N	S

Change the word from GRASS to LAWNS. Change one letter each time, so that each step forms a new word.

· BLUE ANAGRAMS ·

BOIL ALE   _____

CROWN OR ELF   _____

ANY HITCH?   _____

A NERDY HAG   _____

AIR SCUM   _____

CAB OASIS   _____

NAIL GEL   _____

A PAGAN'S HUT   _____

79

· GARDEN SHED ·

Nine answers clued in italics, without definition, are items useful for a gardener and commonly found in the garden shed.

Across

1. *Wanting acre for cultivation* (8,3)
7. Element included by horticulturist inspiringly (3)
9. *Pest in front of Maureen* (5)
10. *Pot Don and Alf moved* (5,4)
11. Drunken miser detained by old dry type, not a moderate (9)
12. Insist on crowd (5)
13. Much-loved Labour politician (7)
15. *Some snowdrop evidently* (4)
18. Second sailor is leading character (4)
20. Museum employee, contemptible figure putting back list of duties (7)
23. *Ridge left out beside river* (5)
24. Plant that's largely fine? No lie possibly (9)
26. *Rod largely I'd plunged into water* (9)
27. Watch perhaps first sign of marigolds appearing in row (5)
28. Nearly omit piece of winter sports equipment (3)

Down

1. Cold fellow in representation of Wilde's old US comedian (1,1,6)
2. Play with second politician – and film (3,5)
3. River located by hard individual? Foreign river (5)
4. Small amount of spirit quietly turning up in horse taking short rest (7)
5. Talk beginning to captivate mad type? (7)
6. Basis for correspondence school that's set up exam (9)
7. *It's drier around end of summer* (6)
8. One barely expressing an outlook? (6)
14. Wit I never deployed in formal questioning (9)
16. *First character in spinney in fitter condition* (8)
17. Prime area for theatregoers – and place for props? (5,3)

29. *Welsh type that's slippery beginning to break in tool cutting up ground* (11)

19. About to eat around wife –
    and drink (3,4)
20. Shelter formerly found in
    California (7)
21. Entices casual worker with
    time on Sunday (6)
22. Section in mag assigned for
    top tennis player (6)
25. Additional actor? (5)

· THE INDOOR GARDENER ·

1. *Sedum burrito* has an animal-related common name. What is it?

2. If your orchid produces aerial roots, what should you do with them?
   a) Trim them back
   b) Cover them with compost
   c) Leave them as they are

3. Which colourful houseplant is commonly grown and sold at Christmas time?

4. What is the common name for houseplants of the *Tradescantia* genus?

5. Which part of your mother-in-law features in the name of a houseplant?

6. One of the commonest succulents found as a houseplant is *Crassula ovata*. One of its common names is the jade plant – what is the other?

7. What colour are the flowers of a peace lily?

8. The *Syngonium* has leaves of a distinctive shape, which give it its two common names. Name one.

9. Is the fern palm (*Cycas revoluta*) a fern or a palm?

10. From where does the polka dot plant originate?

11. In the UK it's called the Christmas cactus, but by what other name is this plant known in the US?

12. Which plant features in Frank Sinatra's 'High Hopes'?

13. Which succulent might be useful in the kitchen, as its juice can be applied directly to burns?

14. The philodendron's name comes from the Greek words 'philo' (to love) and 'dendron' (tree). Why is it so named?

15. With a *Dracaena marginata* in your home, which mythical creature are you housing?

16. The asparagus fern is not in fact a true fern. To which family does it belong?

17. According to the Flowers and Plants Association, what is the UK's most popular houseplant?

18. What is the function of the 'pitchers' of the pitcher plant (*Sarracenia*)?

19. Which 19th-century botanist is credited with developing the terrarium, a glass container in which plants can be grown, and after whom it acquires it alternative name?

20. How do you water an urn plant, a member of the *Bormeliad* family popular as a houseplant?

· HERBS FOR COOKING AND HEALING ·

The names of 18 herbs are hidden in the grid. As you find them and
cross them off, list them in the spaces below the grid.

Y	E	X	I	D	T	N	I	M	N	T	B	F	U	N
L	T	P	I	N	Y	U	U	H	O	P	C	H	C	W
E	Z	L	U	A	K	E	M	C	G	R	Y	O	V	O
C	L	Z	F	M	K	L	G	X	A	H	M	L	E	W
I	U	V	T	Z	J	G	D	A	R	F	X	S	E	P
C	F	K	R	E	D	N	A	I	R	O	C	F	R	A
V	A	L	E	R	I	A	N	E	A	O	R	O	L	R
Y	I	N	G	U	Q	J	Y	Z	T	E	B	E	M	S
C	A	J	G	W	H	P	J	R	V	O	N	M	G	L
X	W	B	E	E	T	V	H	E	A	N	M	I	Q	E
B	A	S	I	L	L	H	F	Q	E	M	M	D	Z	Y
S	E	V	I	H	C	I	Y	F	Q	S	E	Q	S	O
B	Z	A	R	Y	B	X	C	M	T	A	X	S	Q	D
B	O	I	L	C	T	B	P	A	E	G	Y	X	O	X
L	Q	I	H	S	W	P	R	B	Q	E	K	M	G	R

——————— ——————— ——————— ———————

——————— ——————— ——————— ———————

——————— ——————— ——————— ———————

——————— ——————— ——————— ———————

——————— ———————

84

· PLUS ONE 5 ·

Each answer is an anagram of the one above, with one letter added. The final, unclued, answer is a plant, flower or shrub.

Numbered cube used in games

Passed away

First name of 'the Eagle' skier

Undeniably

Made broader

· WORDFLOWER 5 ·

Using the letters in the flower, make as many words as you can of four or more letters. Each word must use the letter in the centre and no letter can be used more times than it appears in the flower. Use all nine letters to make the name of a flower or plant.

Goal:
a minimum of 25 words.

9-letter word

– – – – – – – – –

· WALL ·

Eight clues in italics without definition represent different types of the same plant that might be found growing on a wall. Eight shaded cells reveal the name of the plant.

Across

1. Green substance for catching birds (4)

3. Boring set possibly around hotel – such could be suitable for retiring types? (5-5)

10. Stuff on beach additionally clipped footwear (7)

11. Have a second drink taking in sport usually (2,1,4)

12. Arrived at a church surrounded by grass (7)

13. Hear about the Italian bishop in hat (6)

15. Characteristic Italian restaurant found around India (5)

16. *Jill's partner with chap starts to introduce insecticide* (9)

18. Missing leader, trouble's disturbed the French? That can be analysed (9)

21. Fellow with direction for banquet (5)

23. Party bust sadly creating uncertainties (6)

25. Nothing in list of names rousing figure on farm? (7)

27. *Good character close to rockery* (7)

28. Level ground and river with gold (7)

29. *Early lemons for cultivation? Acre cleared* (5,5)

30. *Part of gazebo, a sanctuary, looking westward* (4)

Down

1. *Rural nests disturbed* (10)

2. *Complaint about conservationists accepted* (7)

4. Favourite pretension supported by patient figure – crime committed with help on site? (6,3)

5. Core compassion (5)

6. Practical outlook is found in kingdom (7)

7. *Favour keeping bits of undergrowth round bushes* (7)

8. Recognise day for something to be sown (4)

9. Prestigious quality shown by hoard on top of table (6)

14. *Very first sign of irises caught near rough ground* (6,4)

17. German gent in Cyprus with piece of pastry that is dessert (6,3)

19. Uncomplaining Scot laid out with daughter absent (7)

20. Liberal yet to be troubled about royal freedom (7)

21. Miss MacDonald left regarding roses? (6)

22. Garland, perhaps, made from a plant found around front of trellis (7)

24. Authority gained from essays originally (3-2)

26. Expanded sporting competition (4)

· WHAT AM I? ·

1. I was represented by a lion on television for some years, but in my more usual form I can be flat-leaved or curly. What am I?

2. I belong to the same family as the potato, and more of me are canned than any other fruit or vegetable. What am I?

3. I'm green, I can be grown in summer or winter, I can be eaten raw in salads or cooked, and I was very popular with a famous cartoon character. What am I?

4. I'm carnivorous, and have the distinction of being described by Charles Darwin as 'the most wonderful plant in the world'. What am I?

5. I come in a huge variety of shapes, sizes and colours, and one of my varieties sells particularly well in October. What am I?

6. I'm the national flower of India and sacred to the Buddhist religion. What am I?

7. I'm a common herb with a name that makes me sound wise, although the literal translation of my Latin name is 'to heal'. What am I?

8. I may look like a banana but I'm not as sweet, and I need to be cooked before you can eat me. What am I?

9. We share the honour of representing our country, although we have very different attributes: one of us is pretty and one of us is edible. What are we?

10. I belong to the same family as sunflowers and daisies, but I'm popular (and very common) in a salad. What am I?

11. I can be sweet or sour, and I can appear in a variety of colours. You can sometimes have a second bite of me! What am I?

12. I'm one of your garden helpers and my Latin name means 'little rings' as I have a segmented body. What am I?

13. I'm sometimes called *Primula vulgaris*, but my common name is much simpler, and I'm a pretty harbinger of spring. What am I?

14. I'm an important crop for feeding animals in many parts of the world but you can also sprout me on your windowsill. What am I?

15. I'm smelly but tasty and you're likely to eat me in France – or Transylvania! What am I?

16. I 'spit' on plants but despite the way this deposit is commonly described, I'm not a bird. What am I?

17. I share my colloquial description, winter cherry, with other plants, but I'm the only one with an oriental-sounding common name. What am I?

18. I'm responsible for making plants look green. What am I?

19. I'm the UK's most popular cooking apple. What am I?

20. I'm often referred to as the gardener's friend, but I'm pretty territorial, and even aggressive if needs be. What am I?

· PLANT ANATOMY ·

```
D S S Q L D L S T K T E O M U
A L T T U G Z A A C J L M D E
D L I B Q U Y F P P U O G A J
S U G W P R Q L Y E E I M Z K
D T M X A N T H E R S T A W E
M K A T I H X E X G X E A L O
P E C M H I N P E F K P Y L V
N E T U E L T N A H Q T X H A
N T U S A N W E Y P S U M V R
Q X B X X D D O I U N G O X Y
F Y I U T P J S D Y O V U L E
A L S M T Z T L E P R A C M J
E A W K C I B H T O P N Y R O
L C S K L T O O R N G C D Z K
N K Q J Z E E O I P Q A M U I
```

Sepal	Axil	Stem	Bud
Anther	Root	Stamen	Pistil
Calyx	Ovule	Ovary	Carpel
Style	Petal	Leaf	
Petiole	Nectary	Stigma	

· RAIN, RAIN, GO AWAY ·

Marion, Debbie, Stan, Bob and Denise were all out working on their allotments when there was a sudden cloudburst. None of them was anywhere near a tree or shed, and yet not a single person got wet. How was this possible?

· WORD FILL 5 ·

Find a four-letter word (which is garden or plant related) that completes each trio of longer words.

1. SY _ _ _ _ ATIC / PEN _ _ _ _ ON / DI _ _ _ _ PER

2. CHI _ _ _ _ RY / BUC _ _ _ _ ER / HURRI _ _ _ _ S

3. S _ _ _ _ ED / TRI _ _ _ _ ERED / A _ _ _ _ S

4. NEW _ _ _ _ NT / SAU _ _ _ _ S / PAS _ _ _ _ WAY

5. LEAT _ _ _ _ ACK / S _ _ _ _ ET / MOT _ _ _ _ OARD

91

· RIDDLED GARDEN ·

In these rhymes, the clues you'll find
They're riddles of the simple kind

Across

1. Shrubs with flowers of pink
   or blue; a feed of rust can
   change the hue (10)

7. Pertaining to 'not made by
   man', created as God only
   can (7)

8. Like some marks on stones
   you find; could be of the
   ancient kind (5)

10. Water all around your plot,
    will make one of these like as
    not (4)

11. If for water you have space,
    this feature will your garden
    grace (8)

13. A time for bonnets, eggs to
    share, and daffs will pop up
    everywhere (6)

15. If gardening is your thing
    to follow, practise, chase, or
    simply wallow (6)

17. Liked by donkeys, so we
    hear, but quite a pain by
    hand to clear (8)

18. From the service tree: a
    berry, not much bigger than
    a cherry (4)

21. White on dark relief of stone
    – a treasure that you maybe
    own (5)

22. For extra foliage to be seen,
    this might describe an
    evergreen (7)

23. Orange, yellow, also red; it
    shows off in a flower bed
    (10)

Down

1. Its garden may not be your
   own, but comfort's here
   away from home (5)

2. It isn't clean but doesn't
   spoil; in your garden's
   known as soil (4)

3. Flowers are such when in
   their prime, just before it's
   seeding time (6)

4. Mostly pink or white or red;
   pot autumn cuttings in the
   shed (8)

5. These will crop up every
   year, like gift books for your
   kids to cheer (7)

6. Controlling growth of nasty
   bugs, but never meant for
   garden trugs (10)

9. England's garden town, it's
   true; or pretty bell in shades
   of blue (10)

12. A root that's cooked and
    eaten cold, or pickled till it's
    very old (8)

14. Evergreen with berries bright
    – all year round a red delight
    (7)

16. Ripe ones good for jam or
    jelly, but early fruit may
    cramp your belly (6)

19. A kind of poppy known to
    yield this substance as its
    name revealed (5)

20. In Latin 'great' this prefix
    found, or skirt that's long
    and near the ground (4)

· TREE–TIME ·

1. Which tree's leaves are the symbol of both the National Trust and the Woodland Trust?

2. Packwood House in Warwickshire contains a famous garden said to represent the Sermon on the Mount. Which trees comprise this garden?

3. Which tree is traditionally regarded as yielding the best sticks for water divining?

4. What is the name given to the art of clipping trees or hedges into ornamental shapes?

5. How old does an oak tree have to be before it starts to produce acorns?

6. Which phrase references a Mediterranean tree, and is used to mean making a peace offering?

7. Which tree species is the world's tallest? Give either the common or botanical name.

8. An adult koala can eat between 200 and 500 grams of leaves each day. Which tree does it favour as its food source?

9. Which traditional custom involves thanking apple trees for the harvest and driving away evil spirits?

10. What is the name of the famous tree in Sherwood Forest, which according to folklore

was where Robin Hood
slept with his Merry
Men?

11. The leaf of which
tree appears on the
Canadian flag?

12. Which variety of fir is
the UK's biggest-selling
Christmas tree?

13. Is the wood of a
coniferous tree hard or
soft?

14. From which country
does bonsai, the art
of growing trees in
miniature, originate?

15. Which three coniferous
trees are native to
Britain?

16. Which tree do we get
turpentine from?

17. Which tree, a 'living
fossil', is native to
Asia and has leaves
that are used to make
supplements to aid
memory?

18. Which tree is the source
of conkers?

19. Which tree is also
known as the holly oak?

20. Which tree traditionally
provided the wood used
in the making of Welsh
'love spoons'?

· ROOT AND BRANCH ·

18 words that relate to trees and woods are hidden in the grid. As you find them and cross them off, list them in the spaces below the grid.

M	E	F	H	B	Y	H	L	T	P	P	O	G	Q	M
Q	A	M	A	W	Y	V	A	B	A	G	Q	O	X	X
L	E	R	C	J	F	M	I	R	S	I	Q	Y	D	I
H	K	L	Y	V	I	X	N	P	D	Y	Q	U	Y	P
C	T	F	G	A	W	A	A	N	T	W	B	L	O	B
N	M	S	L	G	R	B	G	P	I	R	O	T	U	A
A	B	F	E	E	H	N	H	F	U	J	U	O	B	F
R	Z	M	B	R	I	W	O	O	D	L	A	N	D	C
B	J	M	I	R	O	Q	C	C	G	I	W	T	K	O
Y	I	V	A	L	G	F	O	L	O	G	P	C	U	N
T	R	E	Y	C	N	P	G	N	I	N	U	R	P	I
U	L	W	Y	Q	P	C	A	N	O	P	Y	O	X	F
C	P	S	O	I	P	D	B	B	U	W	O	W	P	E
A	P	B	C	E	Q	L	Y	K	M	J	Z	N	I	R
Q	D	E	G	E	R	T	G	N	Q	Z	N	G	C	X

_____   _____   _____   _____

_____   _____   _____   _____

_____   _____   _____   _____

_____   _____   _____

· **WORD LADDER 6** ·

A	N	I	S	E
1				
2				
3				
4				
5				
6				
C	L	O	V	E

Change the word from ANISE to CLOVE. Change one letter each time, so that each step forms a new word.

· **PERENNIAL ANAGRAMS** ·

NO MEN STEP _____

CRIES OOPS _____

AUNTS HID _____

RUIN A GEM _____

I'D RUB CAKE _____

BAIL SET _____

ONE VICAR _____

ARCH MENU MYTHS _____

· WHEELBARROW RACE ·

Starting in the top left corner and reading clockwise is a
quotation (5,7,3,4,3,5,4,5) followed by the first initial
and surname of its author (1,11), which solvers will
know to be all too true!

Across

6. One who resists found amid harebells (5)

7. A good place for rock-plants is around about tool? (7)

8. Outrageous hype noted for plant living within another (9)

9. Heart of willow is sick (3)

10. Might hoarder scold this treedwelling mammal? (8,5)

13. Might fakirs imbibe this – probably not (3)

14. Audibly happy cat is a pest in the garden (9)

17. One who argues with former undisputed middleweight champion, we hear (7)

18. Spouse's relative perhaps is contained within statute (2-3)

Down

1. Went out to knock top from spider's home over border (5)

2. Flower forms from tops of twisted unfurled leaves inside petals (5)

3. *Erythrina lysistemon* might result from something Jack planted? (5,4,4)

4. Woolly red ewes maybe used to remove 14s (7)

5. Prince of Monaco is wetter than usual? (7)

11. Vertical post in garden structure is good and true? (7)

12. Returning to a glade reminds one of the scarlet seaweeds? (3,4)

15. A girl called Heather? Yes and no (5)

16. Is sea lapping everywhere surrounding heads of these lands? (5)

· TRUST IN ME ·

These questions all relate to National Trust gardens in the UK.

1. Which author and poet designed the herb garden at Buckland Abbey in Devon?

2. Which property in Staffordshire features grounds in which you can 'travel' through Chinese, Egyptian and Italianate gardens, amongst others?

3. In the garden of the Churchill family home, Chartwell in Kent, there is a feature called the 'Marycot'. What is it?

4. Which property in Devon, with both house and garden designed by Sir Edwin Lutyens, is sometimes described as 'the last castle to be built in England'?

5. Which property in West Sussex has both a magnolia and a eucryphia named after it?

6. In which East Anglian garden would you find the Coronation Walk, planted to commemorate the coronation of George VI, and a working water mill?

7. Which water garden in Yorkshire, first laid out in the 18th century, now has World Heritage Site status?

8. Who was the 'socialite gardener' of the 1920s and 1930s who designed the gardens for Blickling Estate in Norfolk?

9. Approximately how many varieties of rose would you find in the garden at Mottisfont in Hampshire?

10. In which garden in the south-west of England might you find yourself at the theatre?

11. In which garden in the north of Ireland is there a national collection of penstemons?

12. Which structure is missing from Clumber Park in Nottinghamshire?

13. Which property in Devon, once home to Sir Francis Drake, contains a box-edged garden of medicinal herbs?

14. The garden of Lavenham Guildhall in Suffolk contains plants which would have been grown there in medieval times, such as safflower, madder, cardoon and woad. For what purpose were these grown?

15. In which garden at Mount Stewart in Co. Down would you find a topiary harp?

16. Which property and garden has a connection to a US president?

17. Bodnant in Conwy has a famous 'tunnel' feature, best enjoyed in May and June. Of what is it comprised?

18. Who or what are Adam and Eve at Speke Hall in Liverpool?

19. Which architect and garden designer is responsible for the famous 1920s water garden at Buscot Park in Oxfordshire?

20. Which biblical structure inspired the walled kitchen garden at Trengwainton in Devon?

· EVERGREENS ·

```
R R H V V C X B B P C A Q L P
R H V S Y T H J O K M I B A E
B T O L U P W O X A M L M U U
E L L D R R S V I D C L C R E
W O L I O S D D C S Z E O E G
H I V V E D E O N C Y M T L D
X E T R M N E N O D S A O R E
T C P I H S E N K W W C N C S
D Y V A Q B B C D S I R E I P
C E I Y U C C A U R R Z A N M
Z R M A H O N I A R O T S K L
A H T N A C A R Y P P N T M J
I Y O R E U P L K S D S E C Y
C N E S F Z W U S Q S Y R G B
L D Y W P F V B A E S I O U N
```

Laurel	Box	Choisya	Cotoneaster
Privet	Mahonia	Pyracantha	Yucca
Yew	Maidenhair	Rhododendron	Camellia
Woodrush	Sedge	Pieris	
Cypress	Holly	Spruce	

· PLUS ONE 6 ·

Each answer is an anagram of the one above, with one letter added. The final, unclued, answer is a plant, flower or shrub.

Take a small drink

Filled pastries

Grace or elegance

Enforce or compel

Pledge

· WORDFLOWER 6 ·

Using the letters in the flower, make as many words as you can of four or more letters. Each word must use the letter in the centre and no letter can be used more times than it appears in the flower. Use all nine letters to make the name of a garden friend.

Goal: a minimum of 30 words.

9-letter word

_ _ _ _ _ _ _ _ _

· DISPOSAL ·

Entries clued without definition, in italics, could require 'disposal' by gardeners in a form generating 31 Across (also clued without definition).

Across

8. Pub close to park (4)

9. *African language games lacking substance* (5)

10. and 19. *Lifeless cow found within borders of fields* (4,7)

11. A head linked to old Greek god (6)

12. Affectedly superior boy around hospital I had upset (3-2-3)

13. Diplomatic story tiny bit associated with priest and European (5,3)

15. Take in gradually body of laws (6)

17. Admire greatly international language followed by Elizabeth (7)

19. *See 10.*

22. Large features of roof (6)

24. *See 14 Down*

26. Meal left by a French companion one replaced (8)

28. Activity in amount of work in Eastern US city (6)

30. Design item in garden requiring trimming (4)

31. *Sun attracting donkey* (5)

32. Disturbance in fine American ship (4)

Down

1. Mother beginning to probe gloom (4)

2. Very thin talk Lee's disrupted (8)

3. Saunter in street with swagger (6)

4. Slip, perhaps, if climbing above tree (7)

5. Hope lad's cultivated plant (8)

6. Two fish behaving in lazy fashion (6)

7. Information? A small amount is taken up (4)

14. and 24. *Across Hen nips rugged ground* (5,8)

16. Special equipment needed for small shoot (5)

18. State of uncertainty created by revolutionary American poet mostly (8)

20. Car that's very badly damaged without delay, we hear (5-3)

21. Ordinary wing view (7)
23. Empty tin found in tank (6)
25. Decrepit venue around North is not flat (6)
27. Ill-natured leaders of uncouth group lambasted youth (4)
29. Some disgustingly sudden blast (4)

· ENDLESS VARIETY ·

Each question lists three varieties of a flower, fruit or vegetable. In each case, name what it is that they are varieties of.

1.
January King
Winter White
Christmas Drumhead

2.
Optica
Red Epicure
Crimson Flowered

3.
Worcester Pearmain
Blenheim Orange
Discovery

4.
Dorothy
Edith
Dopey

5.
Harmony
Mozart
Vivaldi

6.
Snowball
Ailsa Craig
Red Arrow

7.
Cavendish
Dwarf Red
Ice Cream

8.
Flamingo
Guyot
Conference

9.
Mrs Cholmondeley
Rasputin
Big Brother

10.
Darcey Bussell
Gertrude Jekyll
Lady Emma Hamilton

11.
Paris Market
Crusader
Thumbelina

12.
Wootton Cupid
Preston Park
Carolina Moon

13.
Czar
President
Victoria

14.
Batavia
Romaine
Escarole

15.
String of Pearls
Cambridge Blue
Crystal Palace

16.
Flamenco
Florence
Finesse

17.
Charantais
Santa Claus
Galia

18.
Golden Lady
Golden Spur
Golden Vale

19.
Black Russian
Moneymaker
Sun Baby

20.
Frills and Spills
Black Satin
Happy Dream

· SPICY PLANTS! ·

The names of 18 spices are hidden in the grid. As you find them and cross them off, list them in the spaces below the grid.

P	C	V	I	A	I	S	J	C	E	F	G	W	T	I
W	V	I	S	L	E	L	I	B	C	X	E	X	Z	J
P	G	K	R	V	L	N	D	D	I	N	M	C	J	F
A	A	I	O	E	N	I	L	A	P	H	T	X	A	Y
P	S	L	N	A	M	R	H	G	S	P	U	E	A	M
R	C	T	M	G	P	R	P	C	L	E	N	W	Z	E
I	K	O	Z	K	E	W	U	P	L	R	A	O	S	M
K	N	Z	V	L	P	R	O	T	A	R	C	Y	F	J
A	S	X	W	Z	P	M	O	M	A	D	R	A	C	K
O	C	B	I	W	E	C	E	C	F	E	N	N	E	L
B	A	Q	B	R	R	D	E	E	S	I	N	A	O	A
F	S	K	T	E	C	M	U	S	T	A	R	D	N	B
Y	S	B	U	F	O	N	I	M	U	C	Z	I	T	L
W	I	C	C	P	R	M	N	P	D	T	S	F	G	C
G	A	U	K	H	N	D	G	C	I	E	Y	E	Q	B

_____   _____   _____   _____

_____   _____   _____   _____

_____   _____   _____   _____

_____   _____

· GARDENER'S DOZENS ·

If there are two dozen onions and you take away three, how many do you have?

· WORD FILL 6 ·

Find a four-letter word (which is garden or plant related) that completes each trio of longer words.

1. G _ _ _ _ IER / B _ _ _ _ ER / F _ _ _ _ OM

2. CE _ _ _ _ A / ARMA _ _ _ _ O / QUESA _ _ _ _ A

3. M _ _ _ _ ATE / TR _ _ _ _ Y / EX _ _ _ _ BATE

4. EN _ _ _ _ S / S _ _ _ _ TCAR / YES _ _ _ _ N

5. EM _ _ _ _ Y / A _ _ _ _ ETIC / TELE _ _ _ _ Y

· OMEN ·

11,4,7,3,8,14 is an old gardeners' saying.

Across

1. This growth enhancer may give lantern oomph! (5,7)
8. Out and out (7)
9. Janitress keeps hold of fertiliser (5)
10. Plant put right amid straggly bush (5)
11. Female cattle possibly – these are blossoming (7)
12. Animal showing reproductive part after losing head (6)
14. Explanation for losing head in treachery (6)
16. With assumed names, earth is surround by a ruined 17 (7)
19. Songbird, lacking distance, might separate the wheat from this? (5)
22. Lily over the pond drives one of these? (5)
23. Destroying tapes that opera singer holds (7)
24. Disturb the harebells to reveal these ericaceous plants (4,8)

Down

1. Prisoner of war found by outskirts of Ypres is here in Wales (5)
2. In the absence of head, teacher is one of the 11 (5)
3. Distress seen in the northern foreign currency (7)
4. Broken foot traps you we hear from a source perhaps (3,2)
5. Saki is a mountain in Scotland (5)
6. Bamboozles footballers with these spices? (7)
7. Use salt in winter? (6)
12. Fit for ploughing, the French horse leads (6)
13. Let this sort out weed (7)
15. An inclination to go topless, may bewitch (7)
17. Agave found by girl and boy, the former being a relative (5)
18. Scandinavian vegetable (5)
20. Disorganised contents from spice drawer? (5)
21. Beech family priest is female not male (5)

· FEATHERED FRIENDS AND CREEPY CRAWLIES ·

1. Which bird is sometimes regarded as a pest because of its habit of eating buds from fruit trees, but is still a popular garden visitor due to the pretty salmon-coloured feathers on its underside?

2. What is the common pond insect that has long back legs covered with fine hairs which it uses like paddles to help it swim?

3. Which small garden bird has the Latin name *Troglodytes* (cave-dweller), although in the garden it will nest in dense vegetation?

4. What do lacewings like to feed on, which makes them a popular form of biological pest control?

5. The collared dove and the wood pigeon have very similar songs. How can you tell the difference?

6. What type of web is woven by the garden spider?

7. What is the other name for the hedge sparrow?

8. This garden insect is called an ear-piercer in French and an ear worm in German. What is it called in English?

9. Which member of the tit family is the smallest European tit?

10. Which beetle can flick itself into the air when disturbed, making a distinctive noise which gives rise to its name?

11. Which bird is celebrated in a 19th-century poem by William Ernest Henley, who describes its song as 'all the joy of life'?

12. It's usually referred to as a daddy longlegs, but what is its correct name?

13. Which is the UK's commonest finch?

14. Buff-tailed, white-tailed and red-tailed are all types of which garden insect?

15. Which bird is Europe's smallest, and has a distinctive gold stripe on its crown?

16. How can you tell a centipede from a millipede at a glance?

17. Which bird's song is often referred to as 'little bit of bread and no cheese'?

18. Where does a mayfly lay its eggs?

19. Which bird rises vertically in the air, flutters in one position whilst singing, and then 'parachutes' back down, always landing on the ground?

20. If you came across a harvestman, you could be forgiven for mistaking it for something else. What does it resemble?

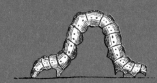

· BEDDING ANNUALS ·

```
M U C A C D Q G E A K O S I G
F U V A P O E Y N Q S L N N C
A T I L L R S A Q T T D E O T
H I D T A E I M E B A M I F N
W L L N R T N O O N X A T N P
W D I E O U S D E S P R A R C
W U U C B P T B U H A I P A K
M F I L E O R S L L K G M I G
N N X R A E L O A P A O I N F
T T M A V P X A X N S L B U Z
M U N I H R R I T N A D I T I
M R U D B E C K I A J R S E N
A I N O G E B D A H L I A P N
B K A R E T S A G W P Q C P I
E D M B A W I N D N V A T M A
```

Dahlia	Marigold	Zinnia	Calendula
Begonia	Geranium	Osteospermum	Nasturtium
Lobelia	Cosmos	Verbena	Aster
Petunia	Phlox	Rudbeckia	
Impatiens	Nicotiana	Antirrhinum	

· WORD LADDER 7 ·

P	E	A	C	H
1				
2				
3				
4				
5				
6				
7				
S	T	O	N	E

Change the word from PEACH to STONE. Change one letter each time, so that each step forms a new word.

· GARDEN TOOLS ANAGRAMS ·

SUET RACES   _____

MR/MRS TIE   _____

BARE FELLOW   _____

NEW AT RACING   _____

PROPELS   _____

A FIR CRIES   _____

GENDER LAW   _____

NEW ARM OWL   _____

· A BOUQUET GARNI ·

The answers to the clues in italics are the names of herbs or
flavourings; these clues do not contain a definition.
The remainder of the clues are normal.

Across

1. *Man with anger* (6)
4. *Sound as if you're invited indoors* (6)
8. Bare people dancing stun Sid (7)
10. Wander across diamond chasm (5)
11. Every knee aches inside (4)
12. To distress Reg I gave a knocking about (8)
14. *Democrat is unwell* (4)
15. *A million to one* (4)
20. To the French rating is wrong with cheese (2,6)
22. Set up equipment in front of a capital (4)
24. Period of time to muse (5)
25. Flattered amphibian that is dead (7)
26. *Annoyed about river line* (6)
27. *Boy returns after drink* (6)

Down

1. *Gordon perhaps?* (6)
2. Mussolini in colour grew less (7)
3. Cut grand tree (4)
5. Subordinate situation for floor covering (8)
6. I hide in surplus fabric (5)
7. *Head girl?* (6)
9. *Small time clever man* (4)
13. Unfortunately loan cape to gangster (2,6)
16. Boy with sex appeal in Gabon needs supervising (7)
17. *Dances playfully* (6)
18. *Make money* (4)
19. *Crosser and nuttier?* (6)
21. Part of egg found in German retreat (5)
23. With pad I dry bed (4)

· GENERAL KNOWLEDGE 3 ·

1. Which root vegetable is also known as the oyster plant?

2. Which tree's name, from Old English words, means literally 'hard tree'?

3. What do laburnum seeds and mistletoe berries have in common?

4. What was originally known as the 'love apple'?

5. Brown Turkey is a variety of which fruit?

6. Which gardener published *The Wild Garden* in 1870, in which he put forth his ideas on planting a mixture of trees and shrubs, perennials and bulbs?

7. Which fictional spy used the common name of *Anagallis arvensis* as his pseudonym?

8. What was the real first name of 'Capability' Brown, the 18th-century garden designer?

9. Two members of the daisy family, both with small white flowers, can be grown easily in the garden and both have medicinal uses – one to help sleep and the other to ease migraines. Name one.

10. What is the name for the study of fungi?

11. 'Plashing' is a term used to describe the collecting or gathering of what kind of nuts?

12. Which part of the *Capparis* plant is harvested and pickled to make capers?

13. Mirid bugs are also known as what?

14. What feature of remontant plants might make them desirable in the garden?

15. Which tree yields sloes, commonly used to make flavoured gin?

16. What milestone did the BBC's *Gardeners' Question Time* reach in 1972?

17. Who was the gardener driven to distraction by Peter Rabbit?

18. What is a stolon?

19. In which county is England's largest forest?

20. Which herb is the smallest species in the edible onion genus?

· A DAY IN THE GARDEN ·

Hidden in the grid are 18 things that you might need, or want, when spending a day in the garden. As you find them and cross them off, list them in the spaces below the grid.

F	R	F	S	S	Z	T	L	G	S	H	B	K	W	S
D	E	L	N	J	A	O	R	E	U	W	Z	O	L	U
A	L	A	O	M	Y	N	V	O	V	R	R	E	I	N
R	E	S	T	X	A	O	D	C	W	R	T	C	Z	G
F	E	K	G	U	L	E	O	W	A	E	B	Q	S	L
R	N	K	N	G	P	F	R	B	I	Y	L	E	V	A
Z	K	O	I	T	Q	E	L	C	B	C	C	K	T	S
C	U	O	L	A	B	E	L	S	N	A	H	W	P	S
U	B	B	L	T	E	L	I	G	T	U	I	E	Q	E
V	D	M	E	H	L	Q	H	E	F	N	S	T	S	S
S	L	C	W	L	J	T	U	T	E	A	A	D	I	T
W	A	T	E	R	P	R	O	O	F	H	E	O	O	S
O	D	A	T	G	S	R	I	A	H	C	K	C	E	D
T	H	A	M	E	Z	K	D	B	E	P	S	C	V	H
R	K	W	U	S	A	A	Q	P	A	E	W	C	N	D

_____	_____	_____	_____
_____	_____	_____	_____
_____	_____	_____	_____
_____	_____	_____	
_____	_____	_____	

· PLUS ONE 7 ·

Each answer is an anagram of the one above, with one letter added. The final, unclued, answer is a plant, flower or shrub.

Opposite of cold

God of thunder

Value

Tossed

Surname of writer Edith

· WORDFLOWER 7 ·

Using the letters in the flower, make as many words as you can of four or more letters. Each word must use the letter in the centre and no letter can be used more times than it appears in the flower. Use all nine letters to make the name of a flower or plant.

Goal:
a minimum of 30 words.

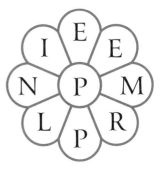

9-letter word

_ _ _ _ _ _ _ _ _

· 'IN THE BLEAK MIDWINTER' ·

The answer to each of the eleven clues in italics, which have no definition, is a plant, or variety of a plant, which can add colour to the garden in winter.

Across

1. *Bearing readjusted round end of Cape* (8)
6. Withdraw intermediate class in some schools (6)
9. Tune I'm rejigging for dance (6)
10. Greek god has the canto forbidden finally in Greek temple (8)
11. *Desert animal lived in Africa first of all* (8)
12. Ann has 50% of ritual happening every twelve months (6)
13. Pals in disarray round leaders of English ensemble in the land of Nod! (6)
16. *Cycle man reassembled* (8)
18. *In Kiev I burn umpteen!* (8)
20. Drink poured out tentatively at first, from this? (6)
22. Boy loses heart after food is dirty (6)
24. Pot roast cooked parts of plants (8)
27. *Relinquish after initially satisfied as things are* (8)
29. *One of five identical children called Emily originally* (6)
30. Removed useless plants, very tiny, one-third disbudded (6)
31. Item of seafood to examine thoroughly in Greek island (8)

Down

2. *Some atmospheric activity* (5)
3. Guy swallowed last of beer before cheese (7)
4. Place of birth? (5)
5. NATO uses it for a letter of the Greek alphabet (5)
6. Enclosure for chickens, for example, in Corunna (3)
7. *Ham hanging up on middle of nail bent upwards* (7)
8. *Very interesting odometer laboratory acquired first of all* (5)
12. Type of necktie from a native of Scotland (5)
14. Footwear found in Erskine (3)
15. *Cooking utensils get messy finally* (5)

16. Irregular projection on revolving shaft can alternate movement first of all (3)

17. Self-confidence, for example, zero! (3)

19. Bound? We could be free (7)

21. *A container for ice cream surrounds it* (7)

23. Enclosed kitchen fireplace in orangery (5)

24. Subject to parking I accept 4th of March (5)

25. Ill-feeling from sly look we hear (5)

26. Unspoken discretion about first of interviews (5)

28. Colour found in ochre dye (3)

· FIVE A DAY ·

1. Name a vegetable that benefits from exposure to winter frost while growing.

2. What is the best type of soil in which to grow parsnips?
   a) Sandy
   b) Stony
   c) Clay
   d) Peaty

3. Which bean is used to make commercial baked beans?

4. What should be added to the soil to prevent clubroot in Brussels sprouts?

5. True or false? The potato and the sweet potato are different varieties of the same plant.

6. What is another name for ladies' fingers?

7. When harvesting beetroot, what is the best way to remove the leaves?

8. Nineteenth-century scientist Gregor Mendel is regarded as the founder of the science of genetics. Which vegetable did he use in his experiments?

9. What is a potato-bogle?

10. When should you plant asparagus crowns?

11. In culinary terms, if a dish is described as 'Florentine' which vegetable will it include?

12. What is the other name for leaf beet?

13. What might cause 'forked carrots' when you grow your own?

14. The United Nations declared 2008 the International Year of ... which vegetable?

15. In which Shakespeare play does a character declare 'If you can mock a leek, you can eat a leek'? (Bonus point if you can name the character!)

16. Garden lore suggests that you should plant shallots on a specific day, and also harvest them on a specific day. Which two days are these?

17. Why might you sow spring onions, mint or leeks alongside carrots?

18. Who first cultivated the potato?
    a) The Celts
    b) The Aztecs
    c) The Native Americans
    d) The Incas

19. Which vegetable is the principal ingredient of borscht, a soup popular in Russia and Poland?

20. What item can be made from the stems of Jersey kale?

· FAMOUS GARDENERS & GARDEN DESIGNERS ·

```
W H G Z V T P R G E M Y E X M
N O T P E R H E O V I Y C A C
I W U W Q E J R T G W U R Q N
O P U L Y J E E O O E X J O F
R D D I P Z O A J W O R S Y D
H S R A M H C T I T E N G J I
N V N E S F I E L D I R E C M
W A L Y A A L U Y B B K C F M
O I N J B Y L Y O T Y R R I O
R R P O E Q E R L L O Y D S C
B P E R D G J B L X B G B H K
E V E N V D N Z U B Q F Q G Z
Q V C T R I Q P E L E H F I C
D Y F C I O A H H X K I V O X
U Y E G A P C Y Q A D Z Z V N
```

Jekyll	Titchmarsh	Peto	Lloyd
Thrower	Corner	Fish	Nesfield
McGregor	Verey	Jellicoe	Page
Repton	Dimmock	Robinson	
Brown	Don	Marx	

· GOING POTTY ·

Gill has some sunflower seeds and some plant pots. If she were to plant one seed in each pot, she would have one pot too few. But if she were to plant two seeds in each pot, she would have one pot too many. How many seeds and pots does Gill have?

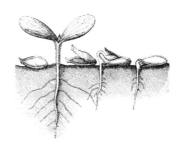

· WORD FILL 7 ·

Find a four-letter word (which is garden or plant related) that completes each trio of longer words.

1. HO _ _ _ _ LY / MI _ _ _ _ RONE / RHI _ _ _ _ ONE

2. S _ _ _ _ MINT / S _ _ _ _ HEAD / REAP _ _ _ _ ED

3. ARC _ _ _ _ D / S _ _ _ _ RING / C _ _ _ _ S

4. TH _ _ _ _ ED / B _ _ _ _ IANT / GUE _ _ _ _ A

5. HO _ _ _ _ ABLE / RE _ _ _ _ E / HO _ _ _ _ AL

127

· RICH PICKINGS ·

'Rich pickings' can be had from the fruits and nuts in unclued answers. Shaded squares form a seven-letter word where the unclued entries as a group could be found.

Across

7. Stretch of water in miraculous place beside lake (5)
8. *Unclued* (9)
10. *Unclued* (6)
11. Addition to salad that's largely smelly I love terribly (5,3)
12. Couple of drugs for unhinged person (8)
13. *Unclued* (4)
15. Plant everyone, say, at home recalled (7)
17. Plant from river found by Greek character working (7)
20. *Unclued* (4)
22. Subsidiary building you once found surrounded by river (8)
25. Drink provided after a form of tripe (8)
26. *Unclued* (6)
27. *Unclued* (9)
28. *Unclued* (5)

Down

1. Clumsy male and young man caught in a riot that's out of control (9)
2. Lane with crab running about? It commonly clings to rocks (8)
3. Cross mostly held by people attending dance (7)
4. Plates I damaged carrying bit of pasta and dried vegetable (5,3)
5. Catmint worried author on reflection (6)
6. Country path ending around river (5)
9. Obstruct promotion of containers for flowers (4)
14. Build unusual court around borders of Nova Scotia – and another (9)
16. Source of fruit with dubious merit in shelter (4,4)
18. Pupil putting nonsense, say, in letter (8)
19. Bachelor in an excited state getting means of eliminating garden refuse? (7)

21. Place for storing food kept
    by irregular dervish (6)
23. Credit gained by criticism?
    Not initially (4)
24. *Unclued* (5)

· FROM BARD TO WORSE ·

Can you identify the missing plant, tree, flower, fruit or vegetable in these Shakespearian quotations? Some of them will be familiar; others you may be able to answer with an educated guess!

1. I know a bank where the wild --- blows
(*A Midsummer Night's Dream*)

2. And there is ---, that's for thoughts
(*Hamlet*)

3. ... why wear you your --- today? Saint Davy's day is past
(*Henry V*)

4. The tartness of his face sours ripe ---
(*Coriolanus*)

5. There's no more faith in thee than in a stewed ---
(*Henry IV, part I*)

6. Hew down and fell the hardest-timber'd ---
(*Henry VI, part III*)

7. With purple grapes, green ---, and mulberries;
(*A Midsummer Night's Dream*)

8. That which we call a --- by any other name would smell as sweet
(*Romeo and Juliet*)

9. To gild refined gold, to paint the ---
(*King John*)

10. I would give you some ---, but they withered all when my father died
(*Hamlet*)

11. The ---, that goes to bed wi' the sun, and with him rises weeping
(*The Winter's Tale*)

12. ... the ---, the more it is
trodden on the faster
it grows
(*Henry IV, part I*)

13. Mine eyes smell ---; I
shall weep anon
(*All's Well That Ends
Well*)

14. Root of --- digg'd i' the
dark
(*Macbeth*)

15. Foolish curs, that run
winking into the mouth
of a Russian bear
and have their heads
crushed like rotten ---!
(*Henry V*)

16. Yes, by Saint Anne, and
--- shall be hot i' the
mouth too
(*Twelfth Night*)

17. A sheep-cote fenc'd
about with --- trees
(*As You Like It*)

18. His reasons are as two
grains of --- hid in two
bushels of chaff
(*The Merchant of Venice*)

19. His wit's as thick as
Tewksbury ---
(*Henry IV, part II*)

20. There is a --- grows
aslant a brook
(*Hamlet*)

· GARDEN ACTIVITIES ·

Hidden in the grid are 18 words that describe things you might do in the garden. As you find them and cross them off, list them in the spaces below the grid.

S	T	K	C	I	P	D	M	F	G	Q	T	A	D	D
B	F	P	I	Z	N	O	W	E	I	Y	W	U	I	D
D	A	P	V	R	V	C	E	R	D	A	C	V	X	B
U	R	B	H	J	R	F	E	T	T	I	I	W	E	X
F	G	S	T	A	K	E	D	I	P	D	O	M	V	I
P	X	V	F	C	D	P	M	L	E	M	N	E	G	O
C	R	G	X	O	U	R	D	I	T	P	O	O	Y	W
T	O	O	R	F	M	T	I	S	R	R	H	O	E	K
H	F	A	P	R	V	C	D	E	P	T	I	Y	F	J
K	K	I	A	A	T	E	N	U	R	P	S	M	O	V
E	V	W	L	N	G	F	P	M	D	R	M	A	Y	I
S	Z	L	A	D	S	A	D	Z	P	E	F	S	J	Z
U	O	L	H	S	L	H	T	D	D	L	R	O	B	M
N	P	P	D	Y	F	L	Z	E	I	O	G	W	L	P
X	W	R	W	F	R	K	S	G	J	H	K	I	A	Y

_____   _____   _____   _____

_____   _____   _____   _____

_____   _____   _____   _____

_____   _____   _____

· WORD LADDER 8 ·

H	I	V	E	S
1				
2				
3				
4				
5				
6				
7				
H	O	N	E	Y

Change the word from HIVES to HONEY. Change one letter each time, so that each step forms a new word.

· SPRING BULB ANAGRAMS ·

SCARS IN US   _____

WORN PODS   _____

FAIRY TRILL   _____

ATE COIN   _____

A CHINK IS UP   _____

HOLLY IVY LEAFLET   _____

LIT UP   _____

DO HOAX ICON   _____

· CUT FLOWERS ·

The answers to the Across clues are all flowers and the clue for each is given as an anagram. To enter start in square no.2 at the top and then continue filling in the Across squares. When you reach the end of row 1 go on to square no.8 and so on until all the Across squares are filled in. The last three letters of the final Across answer cycle to the top and go in the missing three squares in the top row. Each answer begins with the last letter of the preceding one and these letters are already in the grid. Ignore the numbering for these Across clues. The Down clues are normal.

Across

Hail Alec

Tea coin

I slew seed

Worst rat

Get teas

Mae prints

Lit up

In taupe

As mail

A sloe

Lava is

Cash Una

Naves

Lilacs

Down

1. Mildness of fool in a field (6)

2. Sounds like change for table (5)

3. Spa with information element (8)

5. Cows produce these weather terms (4)

6. Fruit eaten by insect for nourishment (7)

7. Muddled story about Eastern mollusc (6)

9. It is on register for tummy trouble (9)

12. Disturb Nile bean for international two year festival (8)

13. Tin in joints all turns to vegetable (7)

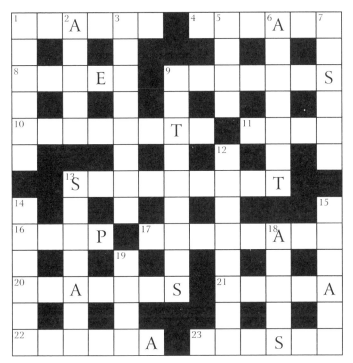

14. Cakes take space on burner (6)
15. Divorce man after light festival (6)
18. Therefore artist returns with victory in afternoons (5)
19. Short top bridge partners make parts of sock (4)

· HERBS AND SPICES ·

1. What is the common name of *Lauris nobilis*?

2. Which spice is used to flavour the drink ouzo?

3. The name of which popular herb stems from the Latin for 'dew of the sea'?

4. What is the culinary term for a bunch of herbs tied together and used to flavour soups and stews?

5. What is the name of the scale used for measuring the spiciness of peppers?

6. Which of the herbs mentioned in the song 'Scarborough Fair' has the Latin name *Petroselinum crispum*?

7. Allspice is not a mixture of different spices – from what part of a plant is it derived?

8. To which family does the coriander plant belong?

9. Which spice is the dried bud of the flower from the tree *Syzygium aromaticum*?

10. How many flowers must be harvested to produce 450g (1lb) of saffron?
    a) 75,000
    b) 500
    c) 10,000
    d) 150,000

11. Which herb acquired the nickname 'knitbone' in traditional herbalism, due to its many uses in healing injuries?

12. Which spice comes in pods that are usually green, but can also be white or black?

13. What was the name of the dog in the children's television series *The Herbs*?

14. Which herb is commonly used in pesto and many other Italian dishes?

15. Why might you sprinkle pepper over your garden?

16. In what form is angelica most commonly used when decorating and flavouring sweet dishes?

17. Which perennial herb with pink or white flowers is often used in remedies to aid restful sleep?

18. In the 17th century a Dutch sea captain recorded that he could smell a particular spice as far away as eight leagues from the shores of Sri Lanka. Which spice, native to the island, was he describing?

19. 'Fines herbes' are often used in French cuisine. The mixture traditionally comprises tarragon, chives and which other two herbs?

20. What colour are the flowers of the curry plant?

· BOTANISTS AND BOTANY ·

```
G C Y M U V F Z N C E A R D S
C I R L A C I P O R T C T I P
K T O H E R B A R I U M E V E
Q O T P P Q E W A Y D S G E C
P X A O A H K U P Q U K P R I
T E V I R L Y B G O R R B S M
S F R F F A M T H O O R Z I E
I E E S T I N S O P L V O T N
N D S R Y A S G A L U A D Y Y
A C N S U A T G E F O I T Q D
T R O K L S A I J R H G Y A X
O P C G T T S D B C Y P Y V C
B I V C E M U I R A R R E T W
F O T A X O N O M Y H Y H Y L
L W O D Z M C G L X P F E R N
```

Herbarium	Botanist	Exotic	Orchid
Phytology	Propagate	Orangery	Catalogue
Fern	Conservatory	Palm	Tropical
Diversity	Habitat	Specimen	
Glasshouse	Taxonomy	Terrarium	

· PLUS ONE 8 ·

Each answer is an anagram of the one above, with one letter added. The final, unclued, answer is a plant, flower or shrub.

Harass, badger

Mum's mum

Scope or extent

Coming from, e.g., Berlin

More shabby

· WORDFLOWER 8 ·

Using the letters in the flower, make as many words as you can of four or more letters. Each word must use the letter in the centre and no letter can be used more times than it appears in the flower. Use all nine letters to make the name of a garden visitor.

Goal:
a minimum of 35 words.

9-letter word

– – – – – – – – –

· GARDEN TOOLS ·

Across

1. Irrigating is able to be done with this garden vessel (8,3)
8. No free-trade island? (5)
10. Charged particle finished early on printing-plate (7)
11. Bishop went round university and hospital in Germany (4)
12. One of two islands one might have obtained suit from? (4)
14. Tree in Tripoli lacking fruit (5)
15. Blades cutting blades (9)
17. Accepts as despatched before Sunday (7)
18. I left dairyman training farmworker (7)
20. Nice area of France (7)
23. More than one plant disease is frustrating (7)
25. Washington terrace with bottom barrel (5,4)
29. In composition four of the quintet rallied (5)
30. Dash to weaken the spirit (4)
31. Border to lean against (4)
32. Sound equipment at that time made of clay (7)

33. Empty search for deep wooded valley (5)
34. Certain iron had been removed from furnace (11)

Down

1. Week cad went to Cumbrian town with handcart (11)
2. Ramblers might be trained on it (7)
3. Reserve some diamonds in fashion centre (9)
4. Blockheads in the soup? (7)
5. Seed vehicle has departed (7)
6. In Louisiana humbled prophet (5)
7. South American river dish (5)
9. Small group in street rioting (4)
13. Directions I am taking to progress through water (4)
16. Tool to give bell-like sound on bridge (4,7)
19. Violently terrorise swaggering person (9)
21. Don't allow doctor round (4)
22. One as a mite, say, living in water (7)
23. Bird pecked another bird (7)

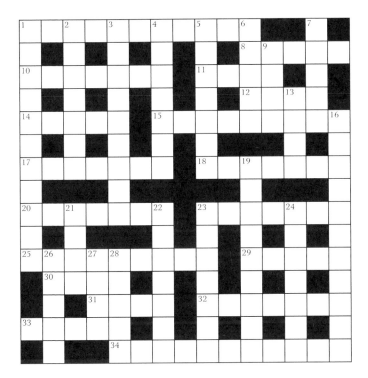

24. Tool buried at end of hostilities (7)
26. A Caledonian course in Berkshire (5)
27. Cheese made round (4)
28. Jewish leader had tailless animal (5)

· THE BUZZING OF THE BEES ·

1. Aside from the queen, what are the two types of bee found in a colony?

2. If you see a small 'volcano' of excavated earth in your lawn, which type of bee might be responsible?

3. On what would a bee larva need to feed in order to become a queen bee?

4. What is the best way to remove a bee sting?

5. Which J.K. Rowling character has a name that means 'bumblebee' in Old English?

6. Which group of pesticides is thought to be responsible for the recent decline in bee populations?

7. How many eyes does a bee have?

8. True or false? Bees are the only insects that produce food for human consumption.

9. What is the purpose of a bee's 'waggle dance'?

10. How many eggs can a queen bee lay in a day?
    a) More than 5,000
    b) 50–60
    c) 1,500–2,500
    d) Around 400

11. Do bees have knees?

12. Male bees can be produced through parthenogenesis. What does this term mean?

13. What is the name given to wine made with fermented honey?

14. What is propolis and for what purpose do bees use it?

15. Why does a bee have two stomachs?

16. If you plant lambs' ears or other downy-leafed plants in your garden, which bee are you likely to attract?

17. Which bees are responsible for the majority of pollination in the UK – bumblebees, honey bees or solitary bees?

18. What causes the familiar buzzing sound of bees?

19. True or false? Bees don't sleep.

20. What is the active compound in bee venom, which causes the burning pain of a sting?

· WEATHER ·

Hidden in the grid are 18 words that relate to weather conditions –
some of which are more welcome to the gardener than others! As you
find them and cross them off, list them in the spaces below the grid.

D	C	S	W	N	G	M	Z	S	N	D	C	U	H	L
Q	O	F	L	O	G	A	T	H	G	U	O	R	D	T
R	M	W	F	E	W	I	R	O	E	H	R	E	O	Z
K	E	P	N	S	E	P	O	W	N	L	X	O	C	Y
F	E	D	R	P	E	T	D	E	A	X	J	W	S	J
S	W	T	N	Z	O	Q	F	R	G	L	V	P	A	L
Y	F	O	E	U	O	U	E	S	N	V	Y	X	K	N
M	Z	E	N	Q	H	N	R	D	I	V	S	U	V	P
Q	R	N	J	S	I	T	R	R	N	T	S	I	M	F
B	K	V	Y	H	C	I	A	X	T	B	S	J	O	R
F	R	O	S	T	Z	I	P	M	H	S	D	N	E	F
N	X	N	Y	Z	N	G	N	Z	G	T	U	D	N	H
H	U	E	L	B	X	D	U	Q	I	O	O	N	W	K
S	H	E	A	T	W	A	V	E	L	R	L	I	P	P
G	W	X	E	I	J	L	M	Y	D	M	C	W	I	M

_____   _____   _____   _____

_____   _____   _____   _____

_____   _____   _____   _____

_____   _____   _____

· PLAYING CAT AND MOUSE ·

Trevor has a problem with mice on his allotment. There are six cats living around the allotment and he's worked out that they can catch six mice in six minutes. How many cats will he need to catch sixty mice in sixty minutes?

· WORD FILL 8 ·

Find a four-letter word (which is garden or plant related) that completes each trio of longer words.

1. COMP _ _ _ _ NT / A _ _ _ _ NTARY/ S _ _ _ _ BALL

2. MI _ _ _ _ HONE / MA _ _ _ _ HAGE / NE _ _ _ _ OLIS

3. AN _ _ _ _ IST / SE _ _ _ _ ED / RESE _ _ _ _ ER

4. HEL _ _ _ _ H / VAR _ _ _ _ S / BAD _ _ _ _ ON

5. T _ _ _ _ DAL / ST _ _ _ _ D / PINST _ _ _ _ D

· GARDENER, HEAL THYSELF! ·

The eleven clues in italics have no definition: the answers
are plants which are generally considered to have healing
properties.

Across

1. *Vera follows little Albert to Nice finally* (4,4)
5. *Leaders of new environmental trust tackle localised education* (6)
9. Tim ran us all over the place for nature-worship (8)
10. Sorted, resorted and kept in reserve (6)
12. It has links made from china (5)
13. *Pale yellow aromatic substance* (5,4)
14. *Droop with fatigue finally* (4)
15. *Begins engraving partially* (7)
19. Pleased reorganisation passed silently (7)
21. Service tree thus, repairing bark initially (4)
24. *An ache ice rectified* (9)
26. *Part of caftan is embroidered* (5)
27. *Investigate by touching round nymania nodes initially* (6)
28. *Mail comes mostly out of order* (8)
29. Flat metal ring for domestic appliance? (6)
30. Sewer Len reconstructed in film concerning recent events (8)

Down

1. *Air can recirculate* (6)
2. Ban bandit (6)
3. Vera, not deterred initially, has redesigned roofed galleries (9)
4. Determine to work out a clue again (7)
6. Consumed some meat (English) (5)
7. Created anew around middle of arboretum in raised levels (8)
8. Spoil part of agenda Ma generated (8)
11. Complacent acquaintances charm you, fawning last of all (4)
16. Arran story almost revised – and told by these? (9)
17. *Abnormally high temperature felt extremely weird first of all* (8)

18. Part of panorama: Chinese engines (8)

20. Bird to avoid? (4)

21. Plant cabbage generally after half of season has gone (7)

22. Look amused about dictionary's second figure of speech (6)

23. Sounds as though you eat this in instalments (6)

25. Relative is good-natured about excuses initially (5)

· RECORD BREAKERS ·

All of these are documented world record breakers – can you guess the stats that won them the accolade?

1. Heaviest carrot
   a) 8.2 kg (18 lb)
   b) 10.17 kg (22.42 lb)
   c) 12.25 kg (27 lb)

2. Fastest-growing plant (a species of bamboo)
   a) 56 cm (22 in) per day
   b) 12 cm (4.7 in) per day
   c) 91 cm (35.8 in) per day

3. Most Brussels sprouts eaten in one minute
   a) 104
   b) 23
   c) 31

4. Living tree with the greatest circumference (a Montezuma cypress)
   a) 36 m (118 ft)
   b) 28 m (92 ft)
   c) 44 m (144 ft)

5. Largest oak leaf
   a) 41 cm (16.14 in) long and 28 cm (11 in) wide
   b) 29 cm (11.41 in) long and 21.3 cm (8.4 in) wide
   c) 24.9 cm (9.8 in) long and 17.23 cm (6.8 in) wide

6. Heaviest lemon
   a) 3.6 kg (8 lb)
   b) 5.26 kg (11.6 lb)
   c) 5.99 kg (13.2 lb)

7. Most rainfall in 24 hours
   a) 1,105 mm (43.5 in)
   b) 1,870 mm (73.6 in)
   c) 2,499 mm (98.4 in)

8. Most juice extracted from grapes by treading (by an individual) in two minutes
   a) 6.9 litres (12.1 pints)
   b) 20.3 litres (35.7 pints)
   c) 14.7 litres (25.8 pints)

9. Smallest documented species of water lily (size of lily pads)
   a) 3–4 mm (0.1–0.15 in) across
   b) 8–12 mm (0.3–0.5 in) across
   c) 10–20 mm (0.4–0.8 in) across

10. Longest beetroot
    a) 6.4 m (21 ft)
    b) 2.6 m (8.5 ft)
    c) 5.3 m (17.4 ft)

11. Tallest climbing rose
    a) 12.8 m (42 ft)
    b) 22.4 m (73.5 ft)
    c) 27.7 m (91 ft)

12. Longest journey on a lawnmower
    a) 1,760 km (1,093 miles)
    b) 23,487 km (14,594 miles)
    c) 15,736 km (9,778 miles)

· FOR FRAGRANCE ·

```
E L K C U S Y E N O H V A R F
T N I C O T I A N A D I I E Y
J E C S V L E X R C E B L W L
L T E H U V A O L N F U O O P
Z I G W L H S V I C C R N L I
Y C L S S E T M E Z R N G F J
T L M A M R S N S N C U A L F
H G I A C A E I A J D M M L E
Y B R L J S L T S I E E G A J
M Y J Y T E Y S N H D I R W R
E B Z O M N H T N I C A Y H Q
E X C A B N G V H X W E S O R
W K M D A P H N E V W P X J H
K A L M G Y R L R B N Q G C D
H N I T Y D T X O M H U L L C
```

Jasmine	Hamamelis	Wallflower	Dianthus
Lavender	Thyme	Viburnum	Stock
Rose	Wintersweet	Daphne	Magnolia
Honeysuckle	Nicotiana	Rosemary	
Lilac	Lily	Hyacinth	

· WORD LADDER 9 ·

Change the word from HOLLY to BERRY. Change one letter each time, so that each step forms a new word.

H	O	L	L	Y
1				
2				
3				
4				
5				
6				
7				
8				
9				
B	E	R	R	Y

· WILDFLOWER ANAGRAMS ·

I MOB UNCLE _____

OWL PICS _____

SO RIPE, MR! _____

WRY OAR _____

CLONE CROCK _____

BERT CUT UP _____

CELLAR BINS _____

LABEL HER _____

· THREE LOVERS ·

Several of the answers, either alone or
in combination with 3, are lovers of 3.

Across

1. Plant at home in 3, or
thrown around? (8)

5. Pondweed provides every
other meal for deejay? (6)

10. Somewhat without light
initially is attractive (7)

11. Recipe with grated viola?
One provides square meal
(7)

12. A National Trust worker?
(3)

13. Parts in 'Bread' we hear (5)

14. Erica initially in pleasant
surrounding is relative? (5)

15. Soldier in front of a plant
(7)

17. 3 is one of the four ancient
ones – so are nitrogen and
phosphorous (7)

19. Interlace the contents of
resplendent wine-rack (7)

21. Two girls (5 and 4) overlap
for a third (7)

23. Contests held here are not
applicable (5)

24. Material found in lonely
crag (5)

26. Meadow amid clearing (3)

28. French, in the month
of flowers, are fine with
skincare brand (7)

29. Furiously dig nuts (4,3)

30. 51 falsehoods on *Nymphaea*
(6)

31. Buttercup – this may
support black bird? (8)

Down

1. Reformed Athos is a 3 lover?
(5)

2. Expression of approval when
top is removed from Sussex
town (5,2)

3. Server loses one essential
fluid (5)

4. *Victoria Amazonica* could be
strangely lit yellow array
(5,5,4)

6. Fragrant plants from city
sellers (9)

7. Ice does strangely limit
bishop's jurisdiction (7)

8. One to enjoy similarly (5)

9. Crier oils visor haphazardly
to reveal blue flag? (4,10)

15. Spurge erupts providing
expression of surprise
therein (3)

16. Mistakenly, I care about one with Eastern heather family (9)

18. Tree with trunk removed is source of infusion (3)

20. Clover is a broken filter holding nothing (7)

22. Columbo with halves of cone switched for one of the 30 (7)

23. Pruning 'legal' is dreadful (5)

25. Off the straight, like Botanical Gardens? (5)

27. Stern examination seen amid plaudits (5)

· UP THE APPLES AND PEARS ·

1. Which apple shares its name with an Asian mountain?

2. True or false? Apple and pear trees belong to the rose family.

3. One of the most popular eating apples, this variety originally had a three-word name, but is now more usually known by one word of three letters. What is it?

4. What is the name given to rough-skinned apples?

5. Originally from the Ukraine, this pear has distinctive striped skin, which gives a clue to its name. What is it called?

6. Which late apple variety is available in October and November, and has a distinctive purple/maroon skin?

7. What is the adjective, often used in anatomical contexts, that means pear-shaped?

8. Which pear variety is the most widely grown in the UK?

9. Several apples have names that contain the word 'pear'. Name one.

10. Which apple might you see in *Grease*?

11. *Malus domestica* is the scientific name for the apple. What does *malus* mean?

12. Which pear shares its name with a high-speed aircraft?

13. Apart from Golden Delicious, there are several other 'golden' apple varieties. Name one.

14. Which pest is likely to be responsible if your young pears start to turn black at the end and drop from the tree?

15. Which French cider apple might you award a star rating to?

16. Which English city features pears on its coat of arms?

17. Crossing Gala and Braeburn apples gave rise to a new variety that shares its name with a musical genre. What is it?

18. What is the fungal disease that can cause disfigured, sunken patches of bark on the branches of apple trees?

19. In the 18th century, a clergyman from Berkshire introduced a French pear variety, which subsequently acquired its very English-sounding name in his honour. What is it called?

20. Which apple variety shares its name with a Flemish painter?

· ORANGES AND LEMONS ·

Hidden in the grid are the names of 18 flowers that are, or can be, orange or yellow. As you find them and cross them off, list them in the spaces below the grid.

E	F	M	R	A	P	S	O	R	N	S	Y	A	J
Y	S	Z	A	I	I	R	M	E	L	A	U	R	G	S
S	B	C	L	R	I	L	W	F	P	S	C	U	E	J
X	U	U	H	M	I	O	H	O	B	T	O	A	J	K
F	T	S	R	S	L	G	T	A	D	U	R	I	L	S
E	X	O	S	F	C	E	O	O	D	R	C	H	M	L
T	S	I	N	I	N	H	S	L	Q	T	T	T	D	I
E	K	U	R	T	C	N	O	Z	D	I	R	Y	A	L
H	S	H	I	I	W	R	Z	L	R	U	K	S	F	Y
W	W	L	R	O	S	E	A	Q	Z	M	Z	R	F	B
V	L	C	O	R	E	Y	V	N	V	I	G	O	O	M
A	B	A	I	M	S	O	C	O	R	C	A	F	D	Q
R	U	D	B	E	C	K	I	A	L	G	D	Q	I	B
U	P	G	M	U	N	R	U	B	A	L	Q	A	L	B
P	N	P	W	T	N	Q	A	V	Y	Q	G	S	Z	U

_____   _____   _____   _____

_____   _____   _____   _____

_____   _____   _____   _____

_____   _____   _____

· PLUS ONE 9 ·

Each answer is an anagram of the one above, with one letter added. The final, unclued, answer is a plant, flower or shrub.

Man's neck accessory

Ritual

Animal's stomach for eating

Band or strip

Robbers at sea

Relates

· WORDFLOWER 9 ·

Using the letters in the flower, make as many words as you can of four or more letters. Each word must use the letter in the centre and no letter can be used more times than it appears in the flower. Use all nine letters to make the name of a flower or plant.

Goal:
a minimum of 32 words.

9-letter word

_ _ _ _ _ _ _ _ _

· LEAFY VEGETABLES ·

The solution to each of the ten clues in italics, which have no definition, is a leafy vegetable.

Across

6. Restrain, we hear, the rule of a monarch (5)

7. Marginal change is frightening (8)

10. *Taxi takes long time round top of Birmingham* (7)

11. British nobleman is exploring Rome initially more ahead of schedule (7)

12. Sewer rat I caught partly wandering (7)

13. They produce pollen from nests Ma rearranged (7)

14. Paid no attention to graded rides reorganised (11)

19. Bone in the arm sounds amusing (7)

21. *Part of hasp in a chain* (7)

23. *Allow cute rearrangement* (7)

25. Repair part of armrest or else! (7)

26. and 15 Down *HQ of European Commission has new growth* (8,7)

27. *Sounds burnt* (5)

Down

1. Bored of decoration inside built of wood (8)

2. Untouched in diplomacy (6)

3. *Rates crews in a different way* (10)

4. *Kronenbourg's first beer* (4)

5. *Part of overspend I verified* (6)

6. *Firework launched at Cape Canaveral?* (6)

8. Mythical sea creature in dream? I'm confused (7)

9. *Charlie rotovated each section superficially at first* (5)

13. Tension following same rearrangement for needlewoman (10)

15. *See 26 Across*

16. A loading realigned slantwise (8)

17. Type of ock splits haphazardly along layers easily first of all (5)

18. Fibre put with dirtier rope Amanda wound last of all (6)

20. Manure has time for nitrobacteria initially to age (6)

22. Main section includes cricket for example (6)

24. Large water jug found in brewery (4)

KNOW YOUR ONIONS

· THIS OR THAT? ·

'Friend or foe' questions relate to an animal or insect that is a 'friend', i.e. beneficial to the garden, or a 'foe' which is in some way harmful.

1. Friend or foe?
   Mole.

2. True or false?
   Rhododendrons thrive
   in acid soil.

3. Friend or foe?
   Lacewing.

4. True or false?
   A banana plant is a
   herb, not a tree.

5. Friend or foe?
   Harlequin ladybird.

6. True or false?
   Pomology is the science
   of fruit growing.

7. Friend or foe?
   Slug.

8. True or false?
   Reindeer moss is so
   called because its
   branching growth
   pattern resembles
   antlers.

9. Friend or foe?
   Aphid.

10. True or false?
    The Latin name of the
    aspen tree translates as
    'delicate poplar'.

11. Friend or foe?
    Honey bee.

12. True or false?
    Raspberries can help
    to relieve hayfever
    symptoms.

13. Friend or foe?
    Woodlouse.

14. True or false?
    Strawberries are not
    fruits.

15. Friend or foe?
    Wasp.

16. True or false?
    Daffodil leaves should
    be cut back once the
    flower has faded.

17. Friend or foe?
    Spider mite.

18. True or false?
    Weight for weight, kiwi
    fruit contains as much
    vitamin C as an orange.

19. Friend or foe?
    Earthworm.

20. True or false?
    Swedes are part of the
    potato family.

· COMING UP ROSES ·

```
G A S O G U R R E A M G V F G
I R D Y G B X R S V P M L Z R
B N O S E N G L I S H O I B A
Z E R U T A I N I M R D U U N
G U N M N H W L Q I O E G R D
R A Z F Y D R I B N B R N H I
X F L B R A C U L M A N I S F
E X R L I A N O D D A I B N L
I I S R I D W R V T F R M F O
D L B Z A C A D A E M B I G R
A F X T R D A V M A R E L C A
Z F U I N D I Z M W Q R C R S
B L H A G R O S D S H A Y J R
F P T B U S H C K H R Y W E N
L S Q E S H B K Z X C V E L R
```

Floribunda	Modern	English	Grandiflora
Miniature	Climbing	Standard	Briar
Rambling	Hybrid	Rugosa	Gallica
Bush	Groundcover	Wild	
Tea	Dwarf	Shrub	

· GREED IS GOOD ·

The Greedy Gardeners' Club had a donation of 100 packets of seeds. The box containing the packets of seeds was passed around the members. The first person took one packet, and each person thereafter took more packets than the person before, until the box was empty. What is the largest number of people that could have been at that club meeting?

· WORD FILL 9 ·

Find a five-letter word (which is garden or plant related) that completes each trio of longer words.

1. OCCU _ _ _ _ _ N / SYNCO _ _ _ _ _ N / EXTIR _ _ _ _ _ N

2. M _ _ _ _ _ MIND / MON _ _ _ _ _ Y / PL _ _ _ _ _ ED

3. ORG _ _ _ _ _ R / GALV _ _ _ _ _ D / HUM _ _ _ _ _ S

4. GR _ _ _ _ _ S / D _ _ _ _ _ D / CRAB _ _ _ _ _ S

5. P _ _ _ _ _ RP / CL _ _ _ _ _ L / GEN _ _ _ _ _ LLY

· TREE-LINED ·

A border of 15 trees can be found starting at the top left
square and moving clockwise. The last letter of each is
highlighted and is the first of the next.
One tree appears twice.

Across

7. Unnamed excavation is earthly (7)

8. Take dish to the French high table (7)

9. Joint Southern Forces? (6)

10. Sort out ordinary seaman's trunks (6)

11. Duck assumes lower position for nocturnal cover (9)

13. Italian lady getting in some Chardonnay (5)

14. I capture young sheep, removing left feet poetically (5)

16. Listed building chap goes in to demolish (9)

18. New York invaded by lice surprisingly, but quite civilly (6)

20. I got involved in bad crash with sedans (6)

22. My radar unexpectedly displays end of Spar (7)

23. Russian aristocrat's wife in a car crash Hertz finally admitted (7)

Down

1. Downbeat after losing love, got turned off (4,3)

2. Borrow some 'mots' possibly? (9)

3. Unblocked, but nothing to write (4)

4. Noisy ape runs amok with mythical flightless bird . . . (9)

5. . . . ape at sea in North–South tides (5)

6. Betrayal from corrupt Senator (7)

12. Past Times shared with former wicked heads? (3,6)

13. Mortality statistic obtained by dissecting heart within date (5,4)

15. Ruler turns charm on (7)

17. Snag somehow eliminated from stabilising Georgian capital (7)

19. Raccoon skin I put on (5)

21. Fix up Macs! (4)

KNOW YOUR ONIONS

· GENERAL KNOWLEDGE 4 ·

1. Which garden pest is known to be particularly fond of hostas?

2. Why is the cruel plant (*Araujia sericofera*) so called?

3. Hydrangeas are often described as one of two types – mophead and what else?

4. Which essential element can lupins 'fix' into the soil?

5. What name is given to the fruit of a rose?

6. Which plant takes its name from the Italian phrase meaning 'beautiful woman'?

7. Which weed is sometimes known as narrow-leaved dock or spinach dock?

8. Which Shakespearean character said 'Let the sky rain potatoes'?
   a) Prospero
   b) Henry V
   c) Falstaff
   d) Oberon

9. True or false? 28g (1oz) of death cap mushrooms can be fatal.

10. Who was the head gardener of Louis XIV of France who developed the gardens at Versailles?

11. Which weed is specifically named, with a legal obligation that its presence must be declared, on the pre-contract Property Information Form used

in the house-buying process?

12. What shape are campanulate flowers?

13. *Lithops*, plants native to dry regions of southern Africa, avoid being eaten by animals by disguising themselves. What do they mimic?

14. In which English county would you find the Eden Project?

15. What term is used to describe a plant trained as a single tall stem topped by a head of branches?

16. The rhizome of the polypody fern (*Polypodium vulgare*) can be used as a culinary flavouring. In which

type of confectionery is it most commonly used?

17. What might a red lily beetle do if you disturb it?

18. Which apple, originally from New Zealand, is the largest single variety of eating apple produced in England?

19. Damselflies and dragonflies are similar, but one of them has four wings that are nearly all the same size and shape, which can help in identifying them. Which one?

20. What was the disease that led to the devastating famine in Ireland in the 19th century?

· ANSWERS ·

p4 – GENERAL KNOWLEDGE 1
1 May tree or hawthorn; 2 Holly; 3 Lemon: the plant's common name is lemon balm; 4 Fuchsia; 5 Fronds; 6 True; 7. Sand, silt, clay and humus; 8 Mulching; 9 c) 1913; 10 *Hamamelis*; 11 Nebuchadnezzar; 12 Laburnum; 13 1800s (1804); 14 The Rosthchilds; 15 They grow partly or wholly in water; 16 Tea; 17 In a pond; 18 Apples or pears; 19 House sparrow; 20 Good Friday

p6 – BEAUTIFUL BLOOMS

p7 – WORD LADDER 1
BEAN – 1 BEAD – 2 BEND – 3 BAND – 4 BANE – CANE

HERBAL ANAGRAMS
Coriander; Oregano; Peppermint; Rosemary; Tarragon; Chamomile; Angelica; Lemongrass

p8 – IN THE SHADE
Across
1 Cleave; 4 Pendulum; 10 Calendula; 11 Gales; 12 Aorta; 13 Chestnuts; 14 Elegans; 16 Silt; 19 Tuba; 21 Mystery; 24 Unholiest; 25 Hosta; 26 Using; 27 Overlooks; 28 Averages; 29 Oxalis
Down
1 Cyclamen; 2 Enlarged; 3 Vinca; 5 Erasers; 6 Digitalis; 7 Lilium; 8 Misuse; 9 Ruscus; 15 Aquilegia; 17 Cesspool; 18 Bypasses; 20 Anemone; 21 Mother; 22 Aucuba; 23 Thrive; 25 Helix

p10 – THE GARDEN YEAR
Jan. Chitting; Feb. Christmas Rose or Lenten Rose; Mar. St David's Day (1st) – Daffodil, leek; St Patrick's Day (17th) – Shamrock, sweet pea (traditionally sown on this day in Australia); Apr. Hazel; May. Tagetes, borage, nasturtium; June. Bolting; July. Tradition says that if it rains

on St Swithin's Day it will rain for the next forty days; Aug. Layering; Sep. Trumpet; Oct. c) 1,054 kg (2,323 lb); Nov. To protect them from damage by pests, specifically the winter moth caterpillar; Dec. Amaryllis

p12 – Can't See the Wood for the Trees

Hawthorn, Hazel, Oak, Holly, Maple, Birch, Willow, Sycamore, Poplar, Aspen, Yew, Alder, Elder, Beech, Rowan, Chestnut, Walnut, Elm

p13 – Plus One 1

Ear; Tear; Earth; Hearth; Heather

Wordflower 1

Note: This is not an exhaustive list. Well done if you found some more obscure words! This applies to all the subsequent wordflower puzzles.

4-letter words: brut, burp, bute, butt, cube, curb, cure, curt, cute, ecru, puce, pure, putt, true, tube, tutu

5-letter words: brute, butte, butut, cruet, cuter, eruct, erupt, rebut, recut, truce, tuber, utter

6-letter words: butter, cutter, putter

9-letter word: BUTTERCUP

p14 – Flowers

Across

1 Grape hyacinth; 10 Uncanny; 11 Triumph; 12 Cyme; 13 Beech; 14 Lily; 15 Hay; 17 Employ; 18 Gardenia; 20 Not; 21 Sweet pea; 22 Peewit; 23 Fir; 24 Rose; 26 Tulip; 27 Cone; 30 Obadiah; 31 Tableau; 32 Winter aconite

Down

2 Rock maple; 3 Pink; 4 Hayley; 5 Autocrat; 6 Iris; 7 Tempi; 8 Butcher's broom; 9 Chrysanthemum; 13 Bay; 15 Hosta; 16 Adder; 18 Goa; 19 New Forest; 20 Nenuphar; 22 Pip; 23 Fistic; 25 Swami; 28 Silt; 29 Oban

p16 – Fruity

1 Hindberry; 2 Viticulture; 3 June drop; 4 It is covered in spikes (it is also known as the horned melon); 5 Hydroponics;

6 To describe a fruit; 7 b) Snake apple; 8 Apricot; 9 Allowing the fruit to over-ripen, even to begin to rot slightly; 10 Durian; 11 Tangelo; 12 Red; 13 92%: count your answer as correct if you guessed within 3% either way; 14 Gooseberry; 15 b) Apple; 16 200: count your answer as correct if you guessed within 20 either way; 17 Raspberry and blackberry; 18 c) The strawberry; 19 17th; 20 Kiwi

p18 – Structures and Features

```
H   P D E H S T           E D E
  C   E B   R             S E C
  R Y R E K C O R         U C A
    A L G N K             O K R
    L E   O C S           H I R
  I       S   L H I       N N E D
  S       U H A   L E G T N
  T       O     T   F E   O
F O U N T A I N H E       R B B P
  A R B O U R N R         G E O A
  D       C     E Z       T   I T
  R       E     A M           I
  I                   G   M     U
B                         U
```

p19 – Baggage Handling

Maggie was carrying seven and Joe was carrying five.

Word Fill 1

1 POT; 2 HOP; 3 PEA; 4 COS; 5 NUT

p20 – Enrichment

Across

1 Fertiliser; 9 Onshore; 10 Dog Rose; 11 Abbot; 12 A Tough Nut; 14 Hoof And; 16 Stipple; 18 And Bone; 20 Compost; 22 Magnesium; 24 Gapes; 25 Dresser; 27 Reawake; 28 Binary Code

Down

1 Fish Blood; 2 Roost; 3 Ireland; 4 Indoors; 5 Egg; 6 Potash; 7 Horn; 8 Nettle; 13 Grimm; 15 Abode; 17 Phosphate; 18 Armada; 19 Eritrea; 20 Comfrey; 21 Tastes; 23 Glen; 24 Guano; 26 Ski

p22 – Common or Garden

1. Mock orange; 2. Ivy; 3. Red hot poker; 4. Catmint; 5. California poppy; 6. Hollyhock; 7. Speedwell; 8. Knotweed; 9. Honeysuckle; 10. Candytuft; 11. Poppy; 12. Globe thistle; 13. Foxglove; 14. Freesia; 15. Broad bean; 16. Cape daisy; 17. Bluebell; 18. Pink; 19. Horse chestnut; 20. Love-in-a-mist

p23

1. *Galanthus*; 2. *Muscari*; 3. *Crocosmia*; 4. *Nicotiana*; 5. *Rosa*; 6. *Tagetes*; 7. *Gypsophila*; 8. *Thymus*; 9. *Viburnum*;

10. *Echinacea*; 11. *Antirrhinum*; 12. *Hypericum*; 13. *Impatiens*; 14. *Erysimum*; 15. *Salvia*; 16. *Lathyrus odoratus*; 17. *Lavandula*; 18. *Myosotis*; 19. *Galium odoratum*; 20. *Buddleia*

p24 – FRUITY FAVOURITES

Damson, Apricot, Peach, Cherry, Quince, Plum, Raspberry, Orange, Pear, Pomegranate, Apple, Blackcurrant, Grape, Lime, Melon, Fig, Banana, Sloe

p25 – WORD LADDER 2

HOPS – 1 BOPS – 2 BOAS – 3 BOAR – 4 BEAR – BEER

TOPIARY ANAGRAMS

Secateurs; Conifer; Pruning; Obelisk; Hedging; Boxwood; Pyramid; Shears

p26 – POETIC GARDENS

Across
5 Honeysuckle; 7 Swan; 8 Radishes; 9 Roland;

10 Edible; 12 Osiers; 14 Potash; 15 Hornbeam; 17 Rail; 18 Resurfacing

Down
1 Inundate; 2 Hybrid; 3 Puddle; 4 Skis; 5 How does your; 6 Everlasting; 11 Intermix; 13 Shears; 14 Pampas; 16 Nest

p28 – TV AND RADIO

1. Bill and Ben the Flowerpot Men; 2. Home Farm; 3. *How Does Your Garden Grow?*; 4. Tommy Walsh; 5. Good; 6. a) Tobacco; 7. Bayleaf; 8. *The Archers*; 9. Guy Cooper, Gordon Taylor; 10. *80 Gardens*; 11. Bob Flowerdew, Pippa Greenwood; 12. *Rosemary and Thyme*; 13. All of them; 14. *Nationwide*; 15. Nigel; 16. False: it is how to control slugs; 17 Percy Thrower; 18. Lyme Park; 19. Diarmuid Gavin; 20. Percy Thrower

p30 – IN THE PINK

p31 – Plus One 2
Tea; Neat; Agent; Eating; Gentian

Wordflower 2
4-letter words: alum, anal, calm, camp, caul, clam, clan, clap, lama, lamp, mana, maul, paca, palm, paua, plan, pula, puma, ulna

5-letter words: canal, clamp, culpa, uncap

6-letter words: alpaca, alumna, lacuna, macula, manual, napalm, panama

7-letter words: almanac, unclamp

9-letter word: CAMPANULA

p32 – Capability Brown
Across

1 Path; 3 Wall; 6 Bench; 10 Retaining; 11 Fence; 12 Insulin; 13 Cleaves; 14 Lawn; 16 Statue; 18 Nod; 21 Yet; 22 Ordain; 23 Uses; 25 Parents; 27 Terrace; 29 Tiara; 30 Lemonades; 31 Oaten; 32 Arch; 33 Pond

Down

1 Partially; 2 Totes; 4 Alienated; 5 Logic; 6 Buffeted; 7 Non-events; 8 Heeds; 9 Viola; 15 Water cart; 17 Triatomic;

19 Dispersed; 20 Fountain; 24 Trunk; 25 Patio; 26 Salsa; 28 Audio

p34 – Garden A–Z
1. Arum lily; 2. Blue poppy; 3. *Callicarpa*; 4. Dogwood; 5. Elephant's ears; 6. Fennel; 7. Ginger; 8. Hazelnuts; 9. Iris; 10. Jacaranda; 11. Kohlrabi; 12. Lime; 13. *Mahonia*; 14. Nutmeg; 15. Orchids; 16. Perennials; 17. Quaking grass; 18. Radish; 19. Scots pine; 20. Turmeric; 21. *Ulex*; 22. Variegated; 23. William Watson; 24. Xylem vessels; 25. Yew; 26. *Zinnia*

p36 – In the Shed

Hoe, Wheelbarrow, Hose, Twine, Seeds, Pots, Fork, Canes, Shears, Compost, Spade, Trowel, Rake, Fertiliser, Bulbs, Trellis, Trug, Mower

p37 – Cabbage Counting

10 – we can call the tomatoes cabbages but that doesn't make them cabbages!

Word Fill 2

1 RYE; 2 SAP; 3 OAT; 4 POD; 5 ASH

p38 – A Thorny Problem

Across

1 Filter bed; 6 Lemon; 9 Reactor; 10 Mahonia; 11 Tree; 12 Recoil; 14 Gas; 16 Outstrip; 17 Acidic; 20 Nepeta; 22 Hawthorn; 25 Fir; 26 Cnicus; 27 Rose; 29 Opuntia; 31 Holdout; 32 Holly; 33 Obnoxious

Down

1 Firethorn; 2 Leanest; 3 Eats; 4 Berberis; 5 Damson; 6 Lah; 7 Managed; 8 Nears; 13 Locate; 15 Static; 18 Concertos; 19 Capuchin; 21 Pursual; 23 Oloroso; 24 Mikado; 25 Froth; 28 Ulex; 30 Try

p40 – Literary Links

1. Quince; 2. *The Constant Gardener*; 3. Triffids; 4. Fleur, Holly; 5. Rosemary; 6. *Cold Comfort Farm*; 7. Harry Potter; 8. The Garden of Eden; 9. Poppy; 10. Tiger-lily, rose, daisy, violet, larkspur; 11. *The Princess and the Pea*; 12. The baobab; 13. Alfred, Lord Tennyson; 14. Rye (*The Catcher in the Rye*); 15. *Tom's Midnight Garden*; 16. *Hamlet*; 17. Kew Gardens; 18. *Nicholas Nickleby*; 19. *Rebecca* (by Daphne du Maurier); 20. A bench in Oxford Botanic Garden

p42 – Garden Friends and Foes

p43 – Word Ladder 3

LEAF – 1 LEAK – 2 LEEK – 3 SEEK – 4 SEEM – STEM

Underground Anagrams

Horseradish; Kohlrabi; Beetroot; Artichoke; Parsnip; Celeriac; Turmeric; Potato

p44 – Plant Crossing

Across

1 Musk melon; 6 Guava; 9 Morus; 10 Mangetout; 11 Cantaloupe; 12 Bean; 14 Pea

bean; 15 Nemesia; 17 Rambler; 19 Filbert; 20 Mast; 22 Eucalyptus; 25 Dandelion; 26 Betel; 27 Cress; 28 Goldenrod

Down

1 Mimic; 2 Strong-arm; 3 Mistakenly; 4 Lampoon; 5 Ninepin; 6 Glen; 7 Above; 8 Attendant; 13 Employable; 14 Paramedic; 16 Spectator; 18 Rousing; 19 Flannel; 21 Singe; 23 Salad; 24 Mess

p46 – FOOD AND DRINK

1. Juniper; 2. A large Asian grapefruit, *Citrus maxima*, also known as a pomelo; 3. Chickpea; 4. Elder; 5. Peach; 6. False: the name means 'little pot'. Poteen is also sometimes distilled from barley grain; 7. Blackcurrant; 8. Avocado; 9. Dig for Victory; 10. Papaya; 11. The stems (usually boiled); 12. Wheat; 13. A silver nutmeg and a golden pear; 14. The seed pod; 15. Apples; 16. Aubergine; 17. Chicory; 18. Perry; 19. Pomegranate; 20. The potato

p48 – HARVEST TIME

```
T I U R F      S H      R          L N
            T A        E A      R
N M U T U A O R        V H E O
D           R V    I      P T C
    L           E E T    I        A
        E          S      R E      G
E   S I        E T            H
L     H Y F  G T              R
K        E        R Y        E
C P I C K A        C A      A   C
I            V S      I P R
S            E      I N O
P R E S E R V E S N      P
W H E A T          G S
```

Sheaves, Autumn, Wheat, Gather, Grain, Festival, Corn, Sickle, Store, Harvest, Ripe, Reaping, Scythe, Crops, Fruit, Yield, Preserve, Pick

p49 – PLUS ONE 3

Era; Real; Early; Parley; Parsley

WORDFLOWER 3

4-letter words: back, bail, bald, balk, barb, bard, bark, bilk, bird, blab, carb, crab, crib, drab

5-letter words: black, brack, braid, brick, rabbi, rabid

6-letter words: bardic, bicarb, bridal, ribald

7-letter word: baldric

8-letter word: baldrick

9-letter word: BLACKBIRD

p50 – POT POURRI

Across

1 Spades; 5 Snails; 10 Cortusa;

11 Astilbe; 12 Rudbeckia;
13 Alcea; 14 Sesame; 16 Fig
trees; 19 Spartium; 20 Garlic;
22 Mulch; 24 Rehmannia;
27 Compost; 28 Sea pink; 29
Cynara; 30 Azalea

Down
2 Paradisea; 3 Drupe; 4 Stalk; 5
Sparaxis; 6 Astrantia; 7 Lilac; 8
Acorns; 9 Cedars; 15 Matthiola;
17 Eglantine; 18 Aubretia; 19
Sumach; 21 Chalky; 23 Limey;
25 Hosta; 26 Azara

p52 – GENERAL KNOWLEDGE 2

1. One that fails to produce
flowers; 2. Mountain ash;
3. Ash; 4. The degree of
fineness of soil particles and its
suitability for root growth; 5.
c) In a gallery – it is a painting
by Van Gogh; 6. Asia; 7.
Harvesting potatoes; 8. Starch;
9. Pomes; 10. Delphinium; 11.
The mole; 12. A one-year-old
tree; 13. Gravel; 14. Bark; 15.
Hairy; 16. Bergamot; 17. Red
maple; 18. Cauliflower; 19.
White blister; 20. b) They are
thorny

p54 – APPLES & PEARS

```
        P     G D K     E         B E
  I Y   I O   C I L         R     M
  R   E L P O   L S H     A       P
  A   D L N P E   T C E           I
  Z E   N M N I E   B O       N R
  N   A   O A B N U     V     A E
      C   G     R R O   J E T
      R       N B   E   O   R
      A W O L G N O O M M N   A Y
  J H O N E Y C R I S P A   P
  M A H R O G G A L A     G C S
                        O
                        L
  R U S S E T           D
```

p55 – WATER WOES

She fills the three-pint can and
empties it into the five-pint
can. She refills it and empties
in another two pints. So she's
left with one pint in the small
can. She then empties the
five-pint can (using it to water
some plants of course) and then
pours her remaining one pint
into the large can. She can then
fill the three-pint can, add that
water to the large can and she
has four pints.

OR

She first fills the five-pint can
and decants three pints into the
small can. She then empties the
small can. She then pours the
remaining two pints from the
large can into the small one.
She can then fill the five-pint

can, pour one more pint into the small can, and have four pints left in her large one.

Word Fill 3

1 TIT; 2 FIG; 3 LOG; 4 DIG; 5 OAK

p56 – A-Mazing

1 Campanula; 2 Agapanthus; 3 Sunflower; 4 Rhododendron; 5 Nigella; 6 Acanthus; 7 Snowdrop; 8 Primrose; 9 Eglantine; 10 Edelweiss; 11 Snapdragon; 12 Nasturtium; 13 Meadowsweet; 14 Thistle; 15 Erica; 16 Aaron's rod; 17 Delphinium; 18 Magnolia; 19 Amaryllis; 20 Speedwell; 21 Loosestrife

p58 – When is a Garden not a Garden?

1. The Garden State; 2. In an octopus's garden; 3. The Garden of Eden; 4. Chelsea Physic Garden; 5. Graeme Garden; 6. The Secret Garden; 7. Common or garden; 8. Operation Market Garden; 9. Covent Garden; 10. In *In The Night Garden*; 11. Garden leave (or gardening leave); 12. *The Garden of Earthly Delights*; 13. Garden of the Gods; 14. The Garden of England;

15. Madison Square Garden; 16. Letchworth Garden City, Welwyn Garden City; 17. Hong Kong Garden; 18. Hatton Garden; 19. Savage Garden; 20. The Garden Route

p60 – Starting From Scratch

Sand, Gravel, Slabs, Fencing, Posts, Topsoil, Hardcore, Edging, Hedging, Turf, Seeds, Plants, Cuttings, Bricks, Mortar, Bulbs, Enthusiasm, Energy

p61 – Word Ladder 4

VINE – 1 WINE – 2 WISE – 3 WISH – 4 WASH – 5 BASH – BUSH

Salad Anagrams

Watercress; Iceberg; Radicchio; Romaine; Spinach; Beansprouts; Escarole; Radishes

p62 – Climbing Fruit

Across

7 Counter; 8 Heroine; 10 Citric; 11 Charmers; 12 Spam; 13 Lie; 14 Sodium; 15 Stone; 17 Smear; 22 Planer; 24 Pie; 26 Rout; 27 Reminder; 28 Notion; 29 Popular; 30 Traitor

Down

1 Apricot; 2 Tamarind; 3 Lychee; 4 Muscatel; 5 Damson; 6 Currant; 9 Peach; 16 Mandarin; 18 Victoria; 19 Morello; 20 Grape; 21 Coconut; 23 Durian; 25 Orange

p64 – Weather Lore

1. Like a lamb; 2. … dry before eleven; 3. Cirrocumulus or altocumulus; 4. 'If the oak before the ash, then we'll only have a splash / If the ash before the oak, then we'll surely have a soak'; 5. Sheep; 6. A white one; 7. … the umbrella maker; 8. A clout is a piece of clothing – the saying is advising against changing from winter to summer clothes too soon; 9. Wet; 10. Weeds; 11. A red sky is caused by high pressure (which usually brings favourable weather) trapping dust in the air, and scattering blue light, leaving the red; 12. Six more weeks of winter; 13. Light reflecting off ice crystals in the atmosphere; 14. April showers; 15. Good – in dry weather the cone dries out and the scales open up; 16. Cumulus; 17.Warm; 18. A good crop ('a load of fruit'); 19. d) The rate at which crickets chirp; 20. A bad one ('coming winter cold and rough')

p66 – National Trust Gardens and Parklands

p67 – Plus One 4

Ale; Bale; Blame; Marble; Bramble

Wordflower 4

4-letter words: afar, fags, fair, fare, fear, figs, fire, firs, frae, frag, refs, rife, safe, serf

5-letter words: afire, fairs, fares, faxes, fears, feria, fires, fixer,

fixes, frags, fries, grief, refix, safer, serif

6-letter words: ferias, fixers, fraise, griefs, safari

9-letter word: SAXIFRAGE

p68 – Bottle-it
Across
7 Banana; 8 Adhere; 9 Sloe; 10 Seedling; 11 Acetone; 13 Limes; 15 Plums; 17 Cowslip; 20 Scot-free; 21 Must; 22 Celery; 23 Lentil

Down
1 Garlic; 2 Date; 3 Damsons; 4 Gages; 5 Chillies; 6 Orange; 12 Tomatoes; 14 Morello; 16 Lychee; 18 Instil; 19 X-rays; 21 Mint

p70 – Weed Woes and Plant Problems
1. Spear thistle; creeping or field thistle; curled dock; broad-leaved dock; ragwort; 2. Damping off; 3. Stinging nettle; 4. It causes a grey mould; 5. *Pissenlit* – 'wet the bed'; 6. Silver leaf; 7. Corsica; it is also known as The Corsican Curse; 8. Leek rust; 9. Eat them, raw or cooked, or made into soup; 10. Mildew; 11. Plant it in a bottomless bucket or pot sunk

into the ground; 12. Beans; 13. a) In the fourth quarter of the moon; 14. Manganese; 15. Stubble burning; 16. Slugs and snails; 17. Bramble; 18. White blister, also known as white rust; 19. Giant hogweed; 20. Raspberry beetle

p72 – Water Gardens

```
T   T   R   Y D   I           B
A   W   E E L   O         U
    D L E E T     F K     F   L
    I P W N   L C N       R   R
    L  K O       I A O O      U
Y   C   N L   N     F R G S
    U   I E       E   P A H
    D     A T       A       R N
P M U P   T         G       O D
        I N         L R
        N U         A E
    G       O P O N D   H
G O L D F I S H E D A C S A C
```

Pond, Koi, Carp, Frog, Tadpole, Fountain, Lily, Bulrush, Algae, Pump, Netting, Filter, Cascade, Dragonfly, Newt, Duckweed, Heron, Goldfish

p73 – An Apple a Day
He gives one of the children their apple in the basket.

Word Fill 4
1 VINE; 2 ROSE; 3 POND; 4 PINE; 5 BUSH

p74 – Show Gardens
Across
1 Hyde Hall; 5 Wisley; 10

Mineral; 11 Chelsea; 12 Tatton Park; 13 Up to; 15 Noticed; 17 Sea mist; 18 Chagrin; 20 Tie beam; 22 Rose; 23 Reciprocal; 26 Isotope; 27 Overuse; 28 Future; 29 Unbeaten

Down

1 Hampton; 2 Donut; 3 Harlow Carr; 4 Lilypad; 6 Iced; 7 List price; 8 Year out; 9 Acorns; 14 Wage freeze; 16 Transport; 18 Cardiff; 19 Nieces; 20 Tricorn; 21 Malvern; 24 Court; 25 Moor

p76 – CONNECTIONS

1. Grapes; 2. Leek; 3. Golden; 4. Cuckoo; 5. Edward; 6. Snow; 7. Dog; 8. Leyland; 9. Hop; 10. Horse; 11. Orchid; 12. Jekyll; 13. Christmas; 14. Sparrow; 15. Creeper; 16. California; 17. Curly; 18. Jerusalem; 19. Jacket; 20. Knot

p78 – THE COTTAGE GARDEN

p79 – WORD LADDER 5

GRASS – 1 GRANS – 2 GRINS – 3 GAINS – 4 PAINS – 5 PAWNS – LAWNS

BLUE ANAGRAMS

Lobelia; Cornflower; Hyacinth; Hydrangea; Muscari; Scabiosa; Nigella; Agapanthus

p80 – GARDEN SHED

Across

1 Watering can; 7 Tin; 9 Flymo; 10 Plant food; 11 Extremist; 12 Press; 13 Darling; 15 Rope; 18 Star; 20 Curator; 23 Edger; 24 Dandelion; 26 Pesticide; 27 Timer; 28 Ski; 29 Wheelbarrow

Down

1 WC Fields; 2 Toy Story; 3 Rhone; 4 Napping; 5 Chatter; 6 Notepaper; 7 Trowel; 8 Nudist; 14 Interview; 16 Strimmer; 17 Front row; 19 Red wine; 20 Conceal; 21 Tempts; 22 Agassi; 25 Extra

p82 – THE INDOOR GARDENER

1. Donkey's tail; 2. c) Leave them as they are, as they help the plant to 'breathe'; 3. Poinsettia; 4. Wandering Jew; 5. Tongue (mother-in-law's tongue, also known as snake plant); 6. Money tree; 7. White; 8. Goosefoot or

arrowhead plant; 9. A fern; 10. Madagascar; 11. Thanksgiving cactus; 12. Rubber tree plant; 13. Aloe vera; 14. In the wild it is a climber that often uses trees for support; 15. Dragon; 16. Lily (*Lileaceae*); 17. Orchid; 18. To trap insects; 19. Nathaniel Bagshaw Ward (the Wardian Case); 20. By pouring water into the 'urn' in the centre of the plant formed by the leaves

p84 – HERBS FOR COOKING AND HEALING

```
Y         D T N I M N
L     I           O               C
E   L       E       G       O
C L           G     A     M     W
I             A R F     E P
C     R E D N A I R O C F A
V A L E R I A N E A O R     L R
Y   N         Y     T E B E S     I
  A   G         R V     N       L
    B   E T       E A N       E
B A S I L L H F   E M       L
S E V I H C I Y F       S E
          C M     A     S
            A E G     E
                          R
```

Rosemary, Parsley, Sage, Basil, Thyme, Dill, Mint, Tarragon, Chives, Comfrey, Feverfew, Valerian, Borage, Cicely, Angelica, Bay, Fennel, Coriander

p85 – PLUS ONE 5

Die; Died; Eddie; Indeed; Widened; Bindweed

WORDFLOWER 5

4-letter words: beer, blub, blue, blur, bulb, burl, burr, bury, byre, lube, ruby

5-letter words: beery, berry, beryl, bluer, bluey, blurb, burly, buyer, rebel, rubel, ruble

6-letter words: blurry, burble, burbly, lubber, rebury, rubber, rubble, rubbly

7-letter word: rubbery

9-letter word: BLUEBERRY

p86 – WALL

The eight shaded cells indicate CLEMATIS.

Across

1 Lime; 3 Night-robes; 10 Sandals; 11 As a rule; 12 Reached; 13 Trilby; 15 Trait; 16 Jackmanii; 18 Resoluble; 21 Feast; 23 Doubts; 25 Rooster; 27 Picardy; 28 Plateau; 29 Nelly Moser; 30 Asao

Down

1 Lasurstern; 2 Montana; 4 Inside job; 5 Heart; 6 Realism; 7 Bourbon; 8 Seed; 9 Cachet; 14 Victor Hugo; 17 Cherry-pie; 19 Stoical; 20 Liberty; 21 Floral; 22 Actress; 24 Say-so; 26 Open

p88 – WHAT AM I?

1. Parsley; 2. Tomato; 3. Spinach; 4. Venus fly trap; 5. Squash or gourd; 6. Lotus; 7. Sage; 8. Plantain; 9. Daffodil and leek; 10. Lettuce; 11. Cherry; 12. Earthworm; 13. Primrose; 14. Alfalfa (Lucerne); 15. Garlic; 16. The nymph of the froghopper; 17. Chinese Lantern / Japanese Lantern (*Physalis alkekengi*); 18. Chlorophyll; 19. Bramley; 20. Robin

p90 – PLANT ANATOMY

```
    S     D L            E
     T   U       A       L
     I B     Y   P P      O
S    G        R        E E  I
 T M    A N T H E R S T        E
 M     A T            E A L O
 E C M             P Y L V
 E T E              T      A
N     S A N        P S        R
 X    X            I          Y
F Y I         S        O V U L E
A L         T L E P R A C
E A     I
L C      L T O O R
```

p91 – RAIN, RAIN, GO AWAY

All of them were married!

WORD FILL 5

1 STEM; 2 CANE; 3 CORN; 4 SAGE; 5 HERB

p92 – RIDDLED GARDEN

Across
1 Hydrangeas; 7 Natural;

8 Runic; 10 Isle; 11 Fountain; 13 Easter; 15 Pursue; 17 Thistles; 18 Sorb; 21 Cameo; 22 Leafier; 23 Nasturtium

Down
1 Hotel; 2 Dirt; 3 Abloom; 4 Geranium; 5 Annuals; 6 Antiseptic; 9 Canterbury; 12 Beetroot; 14 Skimmia; 16 Medlar; 19 Opium; 20 Maxi

p94 – TREE-TIME

1. Oak; 2. Yew; 3. Hazel; 4. Topiary; 5. At least 40 years old; 6. (Offer) an olive branch; 7. Redwood (*Sequoia sempervirens*); 8. Eucalyptus (gum tree); 9. Wassailing; 10. Major Oak; 11. Maple; 12. Nordmann fir; 13. Soft; 14. Japan; 15. Yew, Scots pine, Juniper; 16. Pine; 17. Ginkgo biloba; 18. Horse chestnut; 19. Holm oak; 20. Sycamore

p96 – ROOT AND BRANCH

```
         B    H        P
Q    A        A      A
     R              R S      D
H K              D      U
C T              T W B
N  S     R     G      R O
A B    E E     N        U O
R  M B R I W O O D L A N D C
B    M I R O      C G I W T K O
  I    A L    F O L O G      C  N
T E          P G N I N U R P I
 L          P C A N O P Y O    F
C    I                   W    E R
     C                     N
      E
```

Conifer, Forest, Sap, Bark, Branch, Trunk, Twig, Coppice, Limb, Timber, Canopy, Clearing, Woodland, Bud, Log, Crown, Hardwood, Pruning

p97 – WORD LADDER 6

ANISE – 1 ARISE – 2 PRISE – 3 PROSE – 4 PRONE – 5 CRONE – 6 CLONE – CLOVE

PERENNIAL ANAGRAMS

Penstemon; Coreopsis; Dianthus; Geranium; Rudbeckia; Astilbe; Veronica; Chrysanthemum

p98 – WHEELBARROW RACE

The perimeter reads 'Sweet flowers are slow and weeds make haste' (W. Shakespeare).
Across
6 Rebel; 7 Crevice; 8 Endophyte; 9 Ill; 10 Squirrel shrew; 13 Kir; 14 Dandelion; 17 Haggler; 18 In-law

Down
1 Ebbed; 2 Tulip; 3 Lucky bean tree; 4 Weeders; 5 Rainier; 11 Upright; 12 Red alga; 15 Erica; 16 Isles

p100 – TRUST IN ME

1. Vita Sackville-West; 2. Biddulph Grange; 3. A playhouse designed for Winston Churchill's daughter Mary;
4. Castle Drogo; 5. Nymans; 6. Anglesey Abbey; 7. Studley Royal Water Garden; 8. Norah Lindsey; 9. There are over 500 varieties: count your answer as correct if you guessed within 50 either way; 10. Hidcote (the Theatre Lawn); 11. Rowallane; 12. The house (it was demolished in 1938); 13. Buckland Abbey; 14. To dye cloth; 15. The Shamrock Garden; 16. Washington Old Hall, Tyne and Wear, home of George Washington's ancestors; 17. Laburnum; 18. Yew trees; 19. Harold Peto; 20. Noah's Ark – the garden was built to the supposed dimensions of the ark.

p102 – EVERGREENS

p103 – PLUS ONE 6

Sip; Pies; Poise; Impose; Promise; Primrose

WORDFLOWER 6

4-letter words: meow, thaw, ware, warm, wart, wear, wert, wham, what, whet, whoa, whom, wore, worm, wort

5-letter words: arrow, mower, rawer, rower, threw, throw, tower, water, wheat, whore, worth, wrath, wrote

6-letter words: harrow, marrow, rewarm, warmer, warmth, wormer, wreath

7-letter words: earworm, thrower

9-letter word: EARTHWORM

p104 – DISPOSAL

The entries clued without definition are items of refuse from a garden that could be disposed of in a bonfire and could generate smoke (31 Across).

Across

8 Bark; 9 Twigs; 10 and 19 Dead flowers; 11 Apollo; 12 Lah-di-dah; 13 White lie; 15 Digest; 17 Idolise; 22 Leaves; 26 Luncheon; 28 Energy; 30 Plan; 31 Smoke; 32 Fuss

Down

1 Damp; 2 Skeletal; 3 Stroll; 4 Fielder; 5 Asphodel; 6 Idling; 7 Data; 14 and 24 Across Hedge prunings; 16 Sprig; 18 Suspense; 20 Write off; 21 Opinion; 23 Vacant; 25 Uneven; 27 Ugly; 29 Gust

p106 – ENDLESS VARIETY

1. Cabbage; 2. Broad Bean; 3. Apple; 4. Fuchsia; 5. Potato; 6. Onion; 7. Banana; 8. Pear; 9. Clematis; 10. Rose; 11. Carrot; 12. Dahlia; 13. Plum; 14. Lettuce; 15. Lobelia; 16. Strawberry; 17. Melon; 18. Daffodil; 19. Tomato; 20. Petunia

p108 – SPICY PLANTS!

```
    C   I     S   C E     G
      I   L   E I   C   E
P G     R V L N       I     M C
A   I O E N I       P   T   A Y
P   L N A M   H   S   U   A M
R C   M G P R     C L     N W
I   O       E   U L   A
K N         P   R   T A R
A       P M O M A D R A C
  C         E     C F E N N E L
  A         R D E E S I N A     A
  S       C M U S T A R D     N
  S       O N I M U C       I
  I       R             S
  A       N         E
```

Anise, Chilli, Cinnamon, Peppercorn, Cardamom, Turmeric, Nutmeg, Mace, Allspice, Caraway, Cloves, Cumin, Fennel, Ginger, Mustard, Paprika, Aniseed, Cassia

p109 – GARDENER'S DOZENS
You have the three you took!

WORD FILL 6
1 REED; 2 DILL; 3 ACER; 4 TREE; 5 PATH

p110 – OMEN
The gardeners' saying is 'Flowers out of season, trouble without reason'.

Across

1 Plant hormone; 8 Without; 9 Nitre; 10 Shrub; 11 Flowers; 12 Anther; 14 Reason; 16 Aliases; 19 Chaff; 22 Lotus; 23 Erasing; 24 Bell heathers

Down

1 Powys; 2 Aster; 3 Trouble; 4 Out of; 5 Munro; 6 Nutmegs; 7 Season; 12 Arable; 13 Thistle; 15 Enchant; 17 Sisal; 18 Swede; 20 Anise; 21 Fagus

p112 – FEATHERED FRIENDS AND CREEPY CRAWLIES
1. Bullfinch; 2. Water boatman; 3. Wren; 4. Aphids; 5. The dove's has three 'syllables', the wood pigeon's has five; 6. Orb web; 7. Dunnock; 8. Earwig; 9. Coal tit; 10. The click beetle; 11. Blackbird; 12. Cranefly; 13. Chaffinch; 14. Bumblebee; 15. Goldcrest; 16. Centipedes

have legs that extend from the side of the body, and they are fast runners; 17. Yellowhammer; 18. In water; 19. Skylark (specifically the male); 20. A spider

p114 – BEDDING ANNUALS

```
M  C  C        G  A  O  S
   U  A  O  E  N     S  N
A  I     L  R  S  A  T     E
   I  T  A  E  I  M  E     A  M  I
   L  N  R  T  N  O  O  N     A  T
   I  E  O  U  S  D  E  S  P  R  A
U  C  B  P  T  B  U  H     I  P  A
M  I     E  O  R  S  L  L     G  M  I
   N  R     E  L  O  A     A  O  I  N
      M  V  X     N  L     U  Z
M  U  N  I  H  R  R  I  T  N  A  D     T  I
M  R  U  D  B  E  C  K  I  A        E  N
A  I  N  O  G  E  B  D  A  H  L  I  A  P  N
   R  E  T  S  A              I
                                 A
```

p115 – WORD LADDER 7
PEACH – 1 PEACE – 2 PLACE – 3 PLATE – 4 SLATE – 5 STATE – 6 STALE – 7 STOLE – STONE

GARDEN TOOLS ANAGRAMS
Secateurs; Strimmer; Leaf blower; Watering can; Loppers; Scarifier; Lawn edger; Lawnmower

p116 – A BOUQUET GARNI
Across

1 Borage; 4 Cummin; 8 Nudists; 10 Drift; 11 Each; 12 Aggrieve; 14 Dill; 15 Mace; 20 Au gratin; 22 Riga; 24 Erato; 25 Toadied; 26 Sorrel; 27 Ginger

Down
1 Bennet; 2 Reduced; 3 Gash;
5 Underlay; 6 Moire; 7 Nutmeg;
9 Sage; 13 Al Capone;
16 Editing; 17 Capers; 18 Mint;
19 Madder; 21 Glair; 23 Wadi

p118 – GENERAL KNOWLEDGE 3

1. Salsify; 2. Hornbeam;
3. They are poisonous; 4.
Tomato; 5. Fig; 6. William
Robinson; 7. The Scarlet
Pimpernel; 8. Lancelot; 9.
Chamomile, feverfew; 10.
Mycology; 11. Walnuts; 12.
The flower buds; 13. Capsid
bugs; 14. They flower more
than once in the same year; 15.
Blackthorn (*Prunus spinosa*);
16. Its 1000th episode; 17. Mr
McGregor; 18. An arching or
horizontally spreading stem;
19. Northumberland (Kielder
Forest Park); 20. Chives

p120 – A DAY IN THE GARDEN

```
R F S S   T   G S       W S
E L N   A   R E U     O   U
L A O M   N V O   R R       N
E S T   A O D   W R T       G
E K G   L E   W A E     S L
N K N G     R B I   L E     A
K O I     L C   C C   T S
  O L A B E L S N A H W   S
  B L T E L I G T U I E   E
    E H       E   N S T S S
      W     U E   A
W A T E R P R O O F H
      S R I A H C K C E D
```

p121 – PLUS ONE 7

Hot; Thor; Worth; Thrown;
Wharton; Hawthorn

WORDFLOWER 7

4-letter words: limp, neep, peel,
peep, peer, peri, perm, perp,
pier, pile, pimp, pine, pipe,
prep, prim, ripe

5-letter words: impel, leper,
peril, piler, piper, plier, preen,
prime, primp, repel, ripen

6-letter words: empire, limper,
nipper, nipple, penile, pimple,
prelim, ripple

9-letter word: PIMPERNEL

p122 – 'IN THE BLEAK MIDWINTER'

Across
1 Bergenia; 6 Remove; 9
Minuet; 10 Pantheon; 11
Camellia; 12 Annual; 13 Asleep;
16 Cyclamen; 18 Viburnum;
20 Teapot; 22 Grubby;
24 Taproots; 27 Snowdrop;
29 Quince; 30 Weeded;
31 Crevette

Wellingtons, Gloves, Flask,
Waterproof, Kneeler, Trug,
Secateurs, Labels, Twine,
Gilet, Hat, Wheelbarrow,
Trowel, Sandwiches, Suncream,
Sunglasses, Deckchair, Book

Down

2 Erica; 3 Gruyère; 4 Natal;
5 Alpha; 6 Run; 7 Mahonia;
8 Viola; 12 Ascot; 14 Ski; 15
Pansy; 16 Cam; 17 Ego; 19
Unbowed; 21 Aconite; 23
Range; 24 Topic; 25 Pique; 26
Tacit; 28 Red

p124 – Five a Day

1. Parsnips, or the brassica
family, e.g. Brussels sprouts,
cabbage, kale; 2. a) Sandy;
3. Haricot; 4. Lime; 5. False:
they are unrelated; 6. Okra,
gumbo or bhindi; 7. Twist
them off rather than cutting, to
avoid 'bleeding'; 8. Peas; 9. A
scarecrow, usually with a head
made of a potato; 10. April;
11. Spinach; 12. Chard; 13.
The carrot root growing round
an obstacle such as a stone, or
another carrot planted too close
by; 14. The potato; 15. *Henry
V* (Fluellen); 16. Plant on the
shortest day and harvest on the
longest day; 17. The small of
these plants will deter carrot
root fly; 18. d) The Incas; 19.
Beetroot; 20. Walking sticks

p126 – Famous Gardeners & Garden Designers

p127 – Going Potty

Gill has four seeds and three
pots.

Word Fill 7

1 NEST; 2 PEAR; 3 HIVE;
4 RILL; 5 SPIT

p128 – Rich Pickings

The unclued entries are fruits or
nuts that could be picked in an
ORCHARD.

Across

7 Canal; 8 Raspberry;
10 Walnut; 11 Olive oil;
12 Crackpot; 13 Pear; 15
Nigella; 17 Campion; 20 Plum;
22 Outhouse; 25 Aperitif; 26
Cherry; 27 Blueberry; 28 Peach

Down

1 Maladroit; 2 Barnacle;
3 Gavotte; 4 Split pea; 5 Nepeta;
6 Trail; 9 Stop; 14 Construct;

16 Lime tree; 18 Protegee;
19 Bonfire; 21 Larder; 23 Tick;
24 Apple

p130 – FROM BARD TO WORSE

1. Thyme; 2. Pansies; 3. Leek;
4. Grapes; 5. Prune; 6. Oak;
7. Figs; 8. Rose; 9. Lily; 10.
Violets; 11. Marigold; 12.
Camomile; 13. Onions; 14.
Hemlock; 15. Apples; 16.
Ginger; 17. Olive; 18. Wheat;
19. Mustard; 20. Willow

p132 – GARDEN ACTIVITIES

```
T K C I P       F G           D
F             W E I           I
A             E R D     V
R             E T       I W
G S T A K E D   I     D O
P         C   M L E M
R         U     I T
T   O R     T     S R R H O E
F A P           E T I
  K I     A T E N U R P S M
E     L N G
          A     A           S
      L       T           O
  P           E           W
```

Prune, Trim, Dig, Mow,
Hoe, Weed, Cut, Strim, Sow,
Propagate, Graft, Plant, Rake,
Stake, Pick, Divide, Lift,
Fertilise

p133 – WORD LADDER 8

HIVES – 1 WIVES – 2 WAVES
– 3 SAVES – 4 SALES – 5 SOLES
– 6 HOLES – 7 HONES –
HONEY

SPRING BULB ANAGRAMS

Narcissus; Snowdrop; Fritillary;
Aconite; Puschkinia; Lily of the
Valley; Tulip; Chionodoxa

p134 – CUT FLOWERS

Across
Achillea; Aconite; Edelweiss;
Starwort; Tagetes; Spearmint;
Tulip; Petunia; Alisma; Aloes;
Salvia; Anchusa; Avens; Scilla
Down
1 Lenity; 2 Altar; 3 Hydrogen;
5 Lows; 6 Aliment; 7 Oyster;
9 Enteritis; 12 Biennale;
13 Spinach; 14 Bunsen;
15 Divali; 18 Arvos; 19 Toes

p136 – HERBS AND SPICES

1. The bay tree; 2. Anise
(aniseed); 3. Rosemary –
Rosmarinus: Ros (dew) +
marinus (sea); 4. Bouquet garni;
5. The Scoville Scale; 6. Parsley;
7. A berry; 8. Carrot (*Apiacaea*);
9. Clove; 10. a) 75,000;
11. Comfrey; 12. Cardamom;
13. Dill; 14. Basil; 15. To deter
cats; 16. Crystallised;
17. Valerian; 18. Cinnamon;
19. Parsley and chervil;
20. Yellow

p138 – Botanists and Botany

```
C Y                     D S
  I R L A C I P O R T     I P
  T O H E R B A R I U M E V E
  O T P P   E       S   E C
  X A O A H   U     U   P R I
T E V   R L Y   G O R   S M
S   R       A M T H O O     I E
I   E   T   N S O P L   T N
N   S     A S G A L   A D Y
A   N     A T G E   O I T
T   O   L   A I   R H G A
O   C G   T     B C Y   Y   C
B       E M U I R A R R E T
    T A X O N O M Y H
                    F E R N
```

p139 – Plus One 8

Nag; Gran; Range; German; Mangier; Geranium

Wordflower 8

4-letter words: chid, chin, coif, coil, coin, ding, filo, find, foci, foil, gild, hind, icon, idol, inch, info, lido, ling, lino, lion, loci, loin, nigh

5-letter words: child, chino, cling, dingo, doing, filch, finch, fling, folic, lingo, logic, login

6-letter words: coding, doling, flinch, holing

7-letter words: codling, folding, holding

9-letter word: GOLDFINCH

p140 – Garden Tools

Across
1 Watering can; 8 Atoll; 10 Electro; 11 Ruhr; 12 Uist; 14 Lilac; 15 Lawnmower; 17 Assents; 18 Yardman; 20 Riviera; 23 Blights; 25 Water butt; 29 Tetra; 30 Soda; 31 Abut; 32 Earthen; 33 Coomb; 34 Incinerator

Down
1 Wheelbarrow; 2 Trellis; 3 Reticence; 4 Noodles; 5 Caraway; 6 Nahum; 7 Plate; 9 Trio; 13 Swim; 16 Ring spanner; 19 Roisterer; 21 Veto; 22 Aquatic; 23 Bittern; 24 Hatchet; 26 Ascot; 27 Edam; 28 Rabbi

p142 – The Buzzing of the Bees

1. Drones and workers; 2. Mining bee; 3. Royal jelly; 4. Scrape it, e.g. with a fingernail or bank card; 5. Dumbledore; 6. Neonicotinoids; 7. Five; 8. True; 9. To give other bees information on the location of a good food source; 10. c) 1,500–2,500; 11. Yes and no: they have jointed legs, but no knee cap; 12. Literally 'virgin birth' i.e. reproduction without fertilisation; 13. Mead; 14. A sticky substance formed from tree resin collected by bees, usually mixed with beeswax.

It's used as a 'glue' or 'varnish' to seal small cracks in the hive; 15. One is used for normal digestion; the other is a store for the nectar collected to make honey; 16. The wool carder bee; 17. Solitary bees; 18. Their rapid wing beats; 19. True, though they do rest; 20. Melittin

p144 – WEATHER

Rain, Sunshine, Showers, Fog, Mist, Frost, Clouds, Sleet, Snow, Breeze, Drizzle, Heatwave, Drought, Downpour, Wind, Storm, Thunder, Lightning

p145 – PLAYING CAT AND MOUSE

Six.

WORD FILL 8

1 LIME; 2 CROP; 3 ARCH; 4 MINT; 5 RIPE

p146 – GARDENER, HEAL THYSELF!

Across

1 Aloe vera; 5 Nettle; 9 Naturism; 10 Stored; 12 Chain; 13 Lemon balm; 14 Sage; 15 Ginseng; 19 Elapsed; 21 Sorb; 24 Echinacea; 26 Anise; 27 Fennel; 28 Camomile; 29 Washer; 30 Newsreel

Down

1 Arnica; 2 Outlaw; 3 Verandahs; 4 Resolve; 6 Eaten; 7 Terraced; 8 Endamage; 11 Smug; 16 Narrators; 17 Feverfew; 18 Machines; 20 Duck; 21 Seakale; 22 Simile; 23 Cereal; 25 Niece

p148 – RECORD BREAKERS

1. b) 10.17 kg (22.42 lb)
2. c) 91 cm (35.8 in) per day
3. c) 31
4. a) 36 m (118 ft)
5. a) 41 cm (16.14 in) long and 28 cm (11 in) wide
6. b) 5.26 kg (11.6 lb)
7. b) 1,870 mm (73.6 in)
8. b) 20.3 litres (35.7 pints)
9. c) 10–20 mm (0.4–0.8 in) across
10. a) 6.4 m (21 ft)
11. c) 27.7 m (91 ft)
12. b) 23,487 km (14,594 miles)

p150 – For Fragrance

```
E L K C U S Y E N O H V A R
T N I C O T I A N A   I I E
  E     S   L       R E B L W
L   E   U   A O   N     U O O
I   W   H S V I       R N L
Y   L     S E T M E     N G F
T L   A M R S N S N   U A L
H     I A C A E I A     D M M L
Y     R L I S L T   I     E   A
M     Y     T   E   N   D   R W
E       O M   H T N I C A Y H
      C A             W E S O R
    K M D A P H N E
      A
H
```

p151 – Word Ladder 9

HOLLY – 1 HILLY – 2 HILLS –
3 HALLS – 4 HAILS – 5 HAIRS
– 6 HAIRY – 7 HARRY – 8
MARRY – 9 MERRY – BERRY

Wildflower Anagrams

Columbine; Cowslip; Primrose;
Yarrow; Corncockle; Buttercup;
Cranesbill; Harebell

p152 – Three Lovers

Across

1 Hornwort; 5 Elodea; 10
Sightly; 11 Ravioli; 12 Ant; 13
Roles; 14 Niece; 15 Gunnera;
17 Element; 19 Entwine; 21
Susanna; 23 Arena; 24 Lycra;
26 Lea; 28 Floreal; 29 Like
mad; 30 Lilies; 31 Crowfoot

Down

1 Hosta; 2 Right on; 3 Water; 4
Royal Water Lily; 6 Lavenders;
7 Diocese; 8 Alike; 9 Iris
Versicolor; 15 Gee;

16 Ericaceae; 18 Tea; 20 Trefoil;
22 Nelumbo; 23 Awful;
25 Askew; 27 Audit

p154 – Up the Apples and Pears

1. Fuji; 2. True; 3. Cox; 4.
Russet; 5. Humbug; 6. Spartan;
7. Pyriform; 8. Conference; 9.
Worcester Pearmain, Adams'
Pearmain, Claygate Pearmain;
10. Pink Lady; 11. Bad, evil;
12. Concorde; 13. Golden
Noble, Golden Pippin, Golden
Russet, Golden Spire; 14. The
pear midge; 15. Michelin; 16.
Worcester; 17. Jazz; 18. Apple
canker; 19. Vicar of Winkfield;
20. Rubens

p156 – Oranges and Lemons

```
E   M   A P     P R N S
    S A I R     E   A U
S   C L R I L W   P S C
U U H M I O H O   T O A
T S R S L G T A   U R I
  O S F C E O   D R C H   L
  S I N I N H   L T   T D I
E   U R T C   O   D I   Y A L
S   T I R   L   U   S F Y
    L R O S E A   Z M   R F
            L       N I   O O
A   A I M S O C O R C A F D
R U D B E C K I A         I
    M U N R U B A L   L     L
```

Marigold, Crocosmia, Tulip,
Daffodil, Nasturtium,
Narcissus, Eschscholzia, Rose,
Forsythia, Iris, Sunflower,
Rudbeckia, Dahlia, Primrose,

Crocus, Lily, Potentilla, Laburnum

p157 – PLUS ONE 9

Tie; Rite; Tripe; Stripe; Pirates; Pertains; Spearmint

WORDFLOWER 9

4-letter words: chip, epic, hemp, hump, hype, peri, perm, pice, pier, prey, prim, puce, pure, puri, pyre, ripe, rump, yipe

5-letter words: chimp, chirp, chump, crimp, crump, humpy, hyper, perch, price, pricy, prime

6-letter words: chirpy, cipher, cypher, impure, murphy, pricey, pumice, umpire

7-letter words: humpier

9-letter word: HYPERICUM

p158 – LEAFY VEGETABLES

Across
6 Reign; 7 Alarming; 10 Cabbage; 11 Earlier; 12 Erratic; 13 Stamens; 14 Disregarded; 19 Humerus; 21 Spinach; 23 Lettuce; 25 Restore; 26 Brussels; 27 Chard

Down
1 Timbered; 2 Intact; 3 Watercress; 4 Kale; 5 Endive; 6 Rocket; 8 Mermaid; 9 Cress; 13 Seamstress; 15 Sprouts; 16 Diagonal; 17 Shale; 18 Thread;

20 Mature; 22 Insect; 24 Ewer

p160 – THIS OR THAT?

Note: 'Friend or foe' classifications are generalisations, and may vary according to your personal opinions and experience!

1. Foe; 2. True; 3. Friend; 4. True; 5. Foe: it is not native to the UK and is destroying some friendly native species; 6. True; 7. Foe; 8. False: it is a staple food for reindeer (and is in fact a lichen, not a moss); 9. Foe; 10. False: its name is *Populus tremula*, or trembling poplar; 11. Friend; 12. True: they contain quercetin, a natural antihistamine; 13. Friend; 14. True; 15. Friend; 16. False; 17. Foe; 18. False: it contains approximately twice as much; 19. Friend; 20. False: they are brassicas

p162 – COMING UP ROSES

```
G A S O G U R           F G
  R       G         M L   R
    O   E N G L I S H O   B A
E R U T A I N I M R D   U N
G     N H W L   I   E G R D
A   F Y D R I B   R N H I
  L B R A C U L M   N I S F
  R L I A N O D D A   B   L
  I   R I D W R V T   R M O
D   B A C A D   E     I   R
      D A   A R   L   A
      N             C
      A
  T B U S H
S
```

p163 – GREED IS GOOD

The largest number you could have in the room is thirteen, with the last person taking all the remaining packets. (Person one takes 1, person two takes 2, and so forth until person twelve takes 12, by which time 78 packets have gone. So person thirteen gets the last 22 and becomes the greediest gardener of all!)

WORD FILL 9

1 PATIO; 2 ASTER; 3 ANISE; 4 APPLE; 5 ERICA

p164 – TREE-LINED

The 15 Border Trees are: Yew, Willow, Walnut, Teak, Kumquat, Tea, Ash, Hazel, Lime, Elm Mastich, Holly, Yew, White beam, May

Across
7 Mundane; 8 Plateau; 9 Elbows; 10 Torsos; 11 Eiderdown; 13 Donna; 14 Iambs; 16 Dismantle; 18 Nicely; 20 Chairs; 22 Yardarm; 23 Czarina

Down
1 Went bad; 2 Loanwords; 3 Open; 4 Aepyornis; 5 Neaps; 6 Treason; 12 Old flames; 13 Death rate; 15 Monarch; 17 Tbilisi; 19 Coati; 21 Scam

p166 – GENERAL KNOWLEDGE 4

1. Slug; 2. Because it produces a sticky secretion which (temporarily) traps moths and butterflies, to aid pollination; 3. Lace-cap; 4. Nitrogen; 5. Hip; 6. Belladonna; 7. Wild sorrel; 8. c) Falstaff; 9. True; 10. André le Nôtre; 11. Japanese knotweed; 12. Bell-shaped; 13. Stones; 14. Cornwall; 15. Standard; 16. Nougat; 17. Squeak; 18. Gala; 19. Damselflies; 20. Potato blight